JOHN
GRISHAM

Other Titles in
Critical Companions to Popular Contemporary Writers
Kathleen Gregory Klein, Series Editor

JOHN GRISHAM

A Critical Companion

Mary Beth Pringle

CRITICAL COMPANIONS TO POPULAR CONTEMPORARY WRITERS
Kathleen Gregory Klein, Series Editor

Greenwood Press
Westport, Connecticut • London

Library of Congress Cataloging-in-Publication Data

Pringle, Mary Beth, 1943–
    John Grisham : a critical companion / Mary Beth Pringle.
      p. cm.—(Critical companions to popular contemporary
writers, ISSN 1082–4979)
    Includes bibliographical references (p.) and index.
    ISBN 0–313–29637–5 (alk. paper)
    1. Grisham, John—Criticism and interpretation. 2. Legal stories,
American—History and criticism. I. Title. II. Series.
PS3557.R5355Z82   1997
  813'.54—dc20   96–35026

British Library Cataloguing in Publication Data is available.

Library of Congress Catalog Card Number: 96–35026
ISBN: 0–313–29637–5
ISSN: 1082–4979

First published in 1997

Greenwood Press, 88 Post Road West, Westport, CT 06881
An imprint of Greenwood Publishing Group, Inc.

Printed in the United States of America

The paper used in this book complies with the
Permanent Paper Standard issued by the National
Information Standards Organization (Z39.48–1984).

10 9 8 7 6 5 4 3 2 1

ADVISORY BOARD

Contents

Series Foreword

The authors who appear in the series Critical Companions to Popular Contemporary Writers are all best-selling writers. They do not have only one successful novel, but a string of them. Fans, critics, and specialist readers eagerly anticipate their next book. For some, high cash advances and breakthrough sales figures are automatic; movie deals often follow. Some writers become household names, recognized by almost everyone.

But novels are read one by one. Each reader chooses to start and, more important, to finish a book because of what she or he finds there. The real test of a novel is in the satisfaction its readers experience. This series acknowledges the extraordinary involvement of readers and writers in creating a best-seller.

The authors included in this series were chosen by an Advisory Board composed of high school English teachers and high school and public librarians. They ranked a list of best-selling writers according to their popularity among different groups of readers. Writers in the top-ranked group who had not received book-length, academic literary analysis (or none in at least the past ten years) were chosen for the series. Because of this selection method, Critical Companions to Popular Contemporary Writers meets a need that is not addressed elsewhere.

The volumes in the series are written by scholars with particular expertise in analyzing popular fiction. These specialists add an academic focus to the popular success that these best-selling writers already enjoy.

The series is designed to appeal to a wide range of readers. The general reading public will find explanations for the appeal of these well-known writers. Fans will find biographical and fictional questions answered. Students will find literary analysis, discussions of fictional genres, carefully organized introductions to new ways of reading the novels, and bibliographies for additional research. Students will also be able to apply what they have learned from this book to their readings of future novels by these best-selling writers.

Each volume begins with a biographical chapter drawing on published information, autobiographies or memoirs, prior interviews, and, in some cases, interviews given especially for this series. A chapter on literary history and genres describes how the author's work fits into a larger literary context. The following chapters analyze the writer's most important, most popular, and most recent novels in detail. Each chapter focuses on a single novel. This approach, suggested by the Advisory Board as the most useful to student research, allows for an in-depth analysis of the writer's fiction. Close and careful readings with numerous examples show readers exactly how the novels work. These chapters are organized around three central elements: plot development (how the story line moves forward), character development (what the reader knows about the important figures), and theme (the significant ideas of the novel). Chapters may also include sections on generic conventions (how the novel is similar to or different from others in its same category of science fiction, fantasy, thriller, etc.), narrative point of view (who tells the story and how), symbols and literary language, and historical or social context. Each chapter ends with an "alternative reading" of the novel. The volume concludes with a primary and secondary bibliography, including reviews.

The Alternative Readings are a unique feature of this series. By demonstrating a particular way of reading each novel, they provide a clear example of how a specific perspective can reveal important aspects of the book. In each alternative reading section, one contemporary literary theory—such as feminist criticism, Marxism, new historicism, deconstruction, or Jungian psychological critique—is defined in brief, easily comprehensible language. That definition is then applied to the novel to highlight specific features that might go unnoticed or be understood differently in a more general reading of the novel. Each volume defines two or three specific theories, making them part of the reader's understanding of how diverse meanings may be constructed from a single novel.

Taken collectively, the volumes in the Critical Companions to Popular

Contemporary Writers series provide a wide-ranging investigation of the complexities of current best-selling fiction. By treating these novels seriously as both literary works and publishing successes, the series demonstrates the potential of popular literature in contemporary culture.

Kathleen Gregory Klein
Southern Connecticut State University

The Life of John Grisham

Born in Jonesboro, Arkansas, in 1955, John Grisham has deep southern roots—so deep in fact that he and President Bill Clinton are distant cousins. Grisham's father earned his living as a construction worker during Grisham's early years. The family, including the future writer's mother, four siblings, and himself, traveled throughout the South wherever the father could find work. Although they were poor, the children seemed not to know it because, as Grisham says, he and his brothers and sisters "were well fed and loved and scrubbed" (Hubbard 44). Every town the family settled in, they immediately stopped at the local library where each family member got a new library card and checked out a stack of books. On Sundays they attended the local Baptist church.

At age 12, Grisham and his family settled in Southaven, Mississippi. There he developed into a good student. His eighth-grade teacher saw something special in him, but not necessarily an eager writer (Mathews 80). Most of his energies were channeled into baseball. Although in high school he showed a surprising fondness for John Steinbeck's novels, he says he never cared much for writing. In college he claims not to have taken a course in composition or creative writing, but he acknowledges having earned a "D" in freshman English (Street 33). Following high school Grisham graduated from Mississippi State University (where he majored in accounting), and then he attended law school at the University of Mississippi. At first he planned to become a tax attorney, with "naked greed" as his primary motivation (Martelle "Hot on the Case" C1). However, Grisham's first tax course convinced him to look for another specialty. Tax law, he felt, was awfully complicated and seemed to change daily. Meanwhile, he found in simulated courtrooms that he was "very, very good on my feet," meaning he could think and speak well in court. These skills eventually led him into private practice.

Having graduated and passed the bar exam in 1981, he began practicing law in Southaven but quickly realized he didn't care for his chosen profession. Although he won his first case by claiming self-defense—a client had shot his wife's lover point-blank in the head six times—he wasn't comfortable with the victory. He knew his self-defense argument was weak, since the dead man had "pulled a tiny .22 and fired one shot that bounced off the husband's chest" (Mathews 80). When he switched to civil law, Grisham won "one of the largest damage settlements ever recorded in De Soto County"—on behalf of a boy who had suffered burns over 92 percent of his body in a water heater accident (*Current Biography* 221–224). Even so, Grisham didn't care for the legal profession. He got tired of defending people for very little pay. "And I found myself . . . representing people I didn't really like in cases that were boring. . . . [O]nce I started writing the first book, the law couldn't measure up" (Kaufman "Legions" A10).

In 1983, Grisham ran successfully for the Mississippi legislature. Wanting to help improve education in his state, he served as a Democrat in the Mississippi state senate from 1984 to 1990, but he quit before the end of his second term because "I realized it was impossible to make changes" (Hubbard 44). Having resigned his state senate seat, he refused to run for the U.S. Senate because "senators are expected to shave and wear socks" (Eller A23).

It was during this period that he began writing novels. He also started lying to his wife. Telling her he was driving to Senatobia, Mississippi, to file a deposition, he and a friend would instead sneak off to Oxford, purchase cigars, and drive out to William Faulkner's old farm. During one of these trips Grisham got out a notebook and started to write a novel (Mathews 79). His first book, *A Time to Kill*, began when Grisham happened upon a trial in which a 10–year-old girl testified against a man who had raped her and left her for dead. Grisham obsessed about the case. "I never felt such emotion and human drama in my life," he told an interviewer. He wondered "what it would be like if the girl's father killed the rapist and was put on trial. I had to write it down" (Hubbard 44). He also realized that if the little girl had been his child, "this guy would be dead" (Mathews 80). He worked obsessively for three years on the project, filling bright yellow legal pads with handwritten text. The novel typed and complete, he submitted it to more than 25 publishers before Wynwood Press finally accepted it. He was paid an advance of $15,000, but the number of copies printed was a mere 5,000 and Grisham himself bought 1,000 copies. Following *A Time to Kill* Grisham spent two years writing *The Firm*, a novel that landed mysteriously on the desk of a New York City movie scout who sent it on to Hollywood. Paramount surprised Grisham by buying film rights to the novel for $600,000, preparing the way for a publishers' bidding war. Doubleday won out at $200,000. One measure of *The Firm*'s success is that it has been translated into 27 languages. This kind of success enabled Grisham to close his law office in 1990 so he could devote more time to writing. Unlike fellow legal-thriller author Scott Turow, who continues to practice law and wonders what he would do if he didn't, Grisham (in 1991 at least) seemed happy with his decision: "I was tired of the stress, the clients and most of the opposing attorneys. I'm very happy to be out of it" (Kaufman "Legions" A10). Despite having closed his law office, Grisham continues to take cases occasionally. In April 1995 he reported that he had "sued the Illinois Central Railroad on behalf of an IC employee who was killed on the job. I am lead counsel. . . . We should go to trial in probably late summer or early fall. . . . This may be my last chance to try a case in front of a jury" (Kelly "Grisham" D1).

Grisham wrote his third novel, *The Pelican Brief*, in only 100 days. A first printing of nearly a half-million copies quickly sold out. By March 1993, 1.35 million hardcover copies and 4.5 million softcover copies of *The Pelican Brief* were in print. With two blockbuster novels topping the best-seller list, *A Time to Kill* was reissued in paperback. Although originally it had sold only a few thousand copies, its 1993 sales quickly sprang over the 3 million mark. Grisham recently received more than $6 million from Hollywood for it. Besides receiving near record payment for movie rights to the novel, Grisham for the first time bargained for some control over production of one of his movies. He was a producer and had a say in how the film script was developed.

The Client, another action novel that sold nearly one million copies per month in hardcover in its first three months, followed shortly thereafter. In *The Chamber*, his fifth book, Grisham departed from his usual legal format established in *The Firm*, *The Pelican Brief*, and *The Client*. Although *The Chamber* merits the descriptive term "legal," it is hardly a "thriller." Readers know early on the identity of the killer. The young attorney-hero's life is never in danger. Instead, the novel focuses on the legal process that eventually leads a convicted murderer to the execution chamber of Parchman State Penitentiary in Mississippi. Many reviewers regard *The Chamber* as closest in style and approach to *A Time to Kill*. On the other hand, *The Rainmaker*, Grisham's sixth novel, returns to the legal-thriller format. In the story a reluctantly principled young man barely out of law school confronts a corrupt and powerful medical insurance company. More comical than Grisham's other novels, *The Rainmaker* casts a wry but kindly eye on attorney Rudy Baylor and his clients.

Life for Grisham himself these days is good, but he prefers country to city and the South to anywhere else. Despite owning his own jet and having worldwide book sales, Grisham rarely spends time outside the American South. Until recently he enjoyed being at home, writing in the morning and riding around his 70-acre estate on a tractor or driving into town in his Saab 900 in the afternoon. Grisham's house near Oxford, Mississippi, is a soft yellow Victorian farmhouse, built by his father-in-law and decorated by his wife, Renee, whom he married as soon as he graduated from law school. The property has a swimming pool, tennis and croquet courts, a chocolate Labrador named Bo, and a cat named Mephistopheles. Grisham and his wife have two children, Ty and Shea, with whom Grisham enjoys playing. One of his passions is coaching little league baseball (his son plays on one of the teams). To that end, he built a baseball field in the pasture in front of his house in Oxford. "Each year," he says, "I add to it. Right now we're constructing dugouts. It has a new infield with a new set of bases" ("A League" 4).

Not long ago, "driven . . . by overzealous fans," the family bought a second home: a secluded plantation outside Charlottesville, Virginia (Henderson 33). Too many people were driving by Grisham's farm in Oxford after visiting Elvis Presley's Graceland in Memphis. Grisham attributes his family's normal life to its reclusivity. "We just stay home," he says (Kelly "Not-So-Trying Times" D1).

Success hasn't radically changed the Grishams' family life. As Grisham puts it, "We've gone from very comfortable to very wealthy" (Oldenberg 1). Before moving to their spacious property in Oxford, they lived in a three-bedroom brick house in Southaven, Mississippi, where Grisham practiced law and where "in a good year" he made $125,000. As a novice writer Grisham typed his manuscripts on a Smith Corona word processor in the laundry room of that house. Grisham's 1992–1993 income, according to *Forbes* magazine, was $25 million. He writes now on an IBM clone with WordPerfect in his own private space. Grisham considers writing not an art but a business. He emphasizes *selling*, not *writing*, books. He makes a dollar on every paperback sold and even more for a hardback.

Grisham, who "wears rumpled Dockers, shaves once a week—on Sunday, just before church," recently became publisher of the *Oxford American*, a Mississippi-based quarterly magazine (Mathews 79). He hopes the journal will become the South's first major arts and general interest magazine, featuring southern artists and new departments on southern literature, travel, people, and music.

Many novelists begin writing when they become interested in a character who keeps them awake at night, but Grisham starts when an idea for a plot comes to him, "a strategy he developed after reading a *Writer's Digest* article on rules of suspense." According to *Newsweek*, Grisham wanted to write a "fast" novel, "very entertaining, episodic and highly visual; long on dialogue, short on symbol: a thriller" (Mathews 80). Recently Grisham has undertaken a couple of cinematic projects besides the movie version of *A Time to Kill*. He is also consultant for a CBS series based on *The Client*. In addition, he is composing a screenplay about a male lawyer resisting a seductive female's advances.

Authors of fiction say they often don't know where their characters will take them. Grisham doesn't begin a novel without first getting a go-ahead from his wife, a former English major at Ole Miss. She is a tough critic and "makes those people in New York look like children," he says (Bearden 70). He also prepares a 45–page outline that contains two paragraphs for each chapter, detailing events in that part of the book. Grisham claims his novels are not about setting, as many southern works are. Whereas William Faulkner and Eudora Welty focused on the Deep South, Grisham says most of his novels could be set anywhere. Two exceptions, though, are his first and fifth books. *A Time to Kill* and much of *The Chamber* are set in fictional Ford County, a place similar to Faulkner's famous Yoknapatawpha, the setting for some of the greatest American novels of the twentieth century. Grisham wants to write more Ford County books, but he is often discouraged from doing so. Legal thrillers like *The Firm* seem to sell best.

Grisham's books tend to be about action; as such, they are comparatively free of complex character development, interior monologue, extra detail, and numerous subplots. According to the *Boston Sunday Globe*, Grisham's novels are "plot driven"; you don't have to ponder issues when you read them. The books "speak to our . . . suspicion that no instrument of government is to be trusted and that power, even when it is not absolute, corrupts absolutely." The books use scene well, and the characters speak to each other in "a jazzily terse way." They are fantasies (Winks 96). Some of Grisham's fantasies get a bit zany, however. In an interview he joked: "When I was a lawyer, I spent a lot of time in court-rooms and thought about killing judges. . . . The good thing about writ-ing fiction is that you can get back at people. I've gotten back at lawyers, prosecutors, judges, law professors and politicians. I just line 'em up and shoot 'em" (Kaufman "Law" A16).

For Grisham, writing has become a way of life. He holds himself to two rules. The first is that you can't be in a hurry when you're writing, and the second is that you must write every day if you want to finish a writing project. Grisham reports that when writing the first two books he got up at 5:00 every morning and started work with cup of coffee in hand by 5:30. "I wrote," he says, "with the flu, on vacation, with no sleep, in courthouses when I could sneak off to a quiet room for 30 minutes, in the state capitol building in Jackson." He carried a legal pad in his briefcase and wrote at every chance he got. Whether he's jogging or fishing or bush-hogging (cutting weeds and brush off his land), he's "still thinking about the next scene" (Street 33).

Everyone, it seems, reads Grisham. In fact, syndicated columnist Dave Barry joked in the *Christian Science Monitor* that there must be a Federal Aviation Administration rule that all passengers boarding airplanes have a Grisham novel in their hands. An article about Grisham in *USA Today* notes that half the top executives interviewed in 1993 included Grisham's novels on their summer reading lists ("Summer Reading" B3). If Gris-ham's fan mail is any indication, his readership is two-thirds female and one-third male. Readers range in age between 10 and 96 (Mathews 81).

Grisham's books are especially popular among high school and college students, many of whom are finding his novels on classroom and sum-mer reading lists. "Gone for the most part are the dreaded required reading lists with *The Scarlet Letter* and *Moby Dick* . . . that darkened bright summer days for school kids. Taking their place are 'recom-mended' reading lists as likely to include a best seller by . . . John Gris-ham as a heavy tome by Dickens" (O'Briant "Schools" D1).

Despite his books' popularity and the corpses that occasionally show up in them, Grisham's novels are suitable for younger and older readers alike. Grisham explains that his mother is relatively young and quite healthy. He says he wouldn't write a dirty book as long as she is alive to read it, adding that "I'm not going to write a book I'd be embarrassed for my kids to read in a few years" either (*USA Today* D5). Thus, if sex occurs in a Grisham novel, it usually reads something like "The two had sex"; similarly, violence isn't particularly bloody.

Nevertheless, critic Ray Sawhill reached a grim conclusion regarding Grisham's appeal: it reveals unpleasant things about Grisham's readers. According to Sawhill, "The books are guileless expressions of America's middle class." What this means, he says, is that the books betray the following "desires and emotions" of Grisham's readers: middle-class Americans hope to retire early; like seeing themselves as "wised-up former idealists"; despise the "media, experts and 'sophisticates' in general"; are frustrated that their jobs aren't more appealing; and are anxious about money even though they have plenty (D14).

A question that reviewers frequently quarrel about is: Are Grisham's books any good? That more than 3,000 people showed up for a Grisham book signing in Boca Raton, Florida, prompted a journalist for the *Atlanta Journal* to ponder the difference between "taste" and "judgment" in terms of the public's reading habits, implying that readers of Grisham's books lack both. (Skube N10). Interestingly, Grisham would probably agree, letting readers of his work bear the brunt of shame—or at least responsibility—for what they read. Grisham is no Marcel Proust, but he makes no claims to be. However, those who love Grisham's writing need only compare his success with that of William Faulkner. Faulkner received the Nobel Prize and won two Pulitzers, but each of his first four novels sold about 2,000 copies and the highest he ever rose on the bestseller list was to tenth place with *The Reivers* in 1962.

Probably the correct question isn't whether Grisham's books are any good. Instead readers, writers, and critics alike should be trying to account for Grisham's immense popularity. Why do so many readers hungrily await his next novel? What exactly is the pulse of America that Grisham successfully measures? Although the critic Ray Sawhill might disagree, there are positive reasons for Grisham's appeal. A "wised-up former idealist" rarely loses sparks of hope and humor. Grisham seems aware of this fact in that he successfully acknowledges readers' disappointed ideals, but also their wry expectation that things could get better and that after all, good people are still capable of combating those who are at worst evil and at best misguided. Grisham's heroes are what matter most to the people who read a Grisham novel, not the forces the heroes contend with: racism, a corrupt legal system, big business and big government, polluters, those who believe justice means an eye for an eye, and a faltering health-care system. And although Sawhill regards Grisham's readers as bored materialists, he may have reached that conclusion by reading *The Firm* one too many times.

Whatever we are, Grisham's readers are all of us. All those people reading Grisham on airplanes represent a cross-section of backgrounds, ethnicities, incomes, religions, and levels of education. Among college students, English majors are as likely as business majors to delight in a Grisham novel. People read for many reasons; the same people read for different reasons. Sometimes we read in the hope that books will carry us to new intellectual and emotional depths. At other times we read for rest and, perhaps, for vicarious adventure. Readers can no longer be neatly categorized as those who read great literature and those who read "trash." Categories overlap. We should stand in awe of John Grisham's gift, his ability to give us what we sometimes want.

John Grisham and the
Legal Thriller

THE GENRE OF THE THRILLER

A "thriller," according to Jerry Palmer in H.R.F. Keating's *Whodunit*, "intends to arouse one predominant emotion: the excitement of suspense" (61). Beyond this basic definition, critics disagree as to whether the thriller is a subcategory of crime fiction (along with detective and private eye fiction, police procedurals, suspense novels, gothic mysteries, and spy stories) or a general term for detective, police, spy, and legal fiction. On the one hand, those who regard thrillers as a subcategory of crime fiction (distinguishing, for example, between detective fiction and thrillers) point out that detective fiction emphasizes the solution to a mystery whereas thrillers have a broader range of plots and emphasize physical action. On the other hand, those who think of "thriller" as an umbrella term see in this kind of fiction elements of mystery as well as suspenseful action. According to them, the distinction between detective story and other kinds of thrillers all but disappeared during the 1930s in Raymond Chandler's and Dashiell Hammett's fiction. Called hard-boiled, these works simultaneously emphasized mystery and violence, a criminal who must be identified, and enough hand-to-hand combat to keep readers' fists in their mouths.

No matter whether one thinks of thrillers as a separate subcategory or a general term, it's important to keep in mind that such works of fiction "are always about criminal activity, and focus around a single hero: it is this combination that is their defining feature" (Palmer "The Thriller" 63). And the criminal activity can't be merely illegal. Illegal is not terrible enough. Instead the crime must be immoral, preferably peculiar, and horribly damaging to an individual or group. The lone hero must act in response to criminal behavior, which is usually from

> a mysterious source: as a result, from the beginning, we see things through his [or her] eyes. And this is essential, not only for moral reasons—so that we feel . . . [the hero] is justified— but also in order to create our pleasure in the story: we want suspense, and we can only get suspense if we are 150 per cent on one side, and equally thoroughly against the others, for suspense consists of wholeheartedly wanting someone to suc- ceed against extreme opposition.

In his own book, *Thrillers: Genesis and Structure of a Popular Genre*, Pal- mer fleshes out what a thriller must contain. Besides a sympathetic hero, there must be "professionalism" as the hero's "central attribute." This professionalism involves qualities that enable the hero to "learn and be self-reliant." Palmer argues that there are positive and negative thrillers; in both, professionalism leads the hero into a life of isolation. In the positive thriller, that isolation is depicted as glamorous. In the negative thriller, the isolation is "bleak." In both positive and negative thrillers, the hero reacts to the "unprovoked aggression of thoroughly unpleasant people" and successfully averts a difficulty that is disrupting the world. Although the hero's efforts ought to resolve whatever has created dis- order, they do so only in the case of the positive thriller. "[I]n the neg- ative version one is left with the sense that . . . [difficulties] will crop up again somewhere else, and soon. Concomitantly, the positive thriller closes with the assurance of happiness for the hero, but the negative is unable to hold out any real assurance: it is an open question whether the hero will be happy or not" (Palmer *Thrillers* 51).

The key to both positive and negative thrillers is the excitement en- gendered by both. We enjoy thrillers not because we can't figure out what is going to happen in the end, but because we delight in the clever way in which the hero defeats opposing forces.

> Excitement derives from experiencing these dramatic irrup- tions through the eyes of the hero; his [or her] perspective

dominates the reader's. This is true both morally and physically: morally, insofar as we identify the hero (for as long as we are reading the story, at least) as the source of good in the world; and physically insofar as, even when the narration allows us to see things from the villain's angle, dramatic and significant events are always shown from the hero's side of the fence. (Palmer *Thrillers* 59)

Therefore, even a reader rereading a thriller can delight in it because he or she can reexperience its excitement. Knowing the villain's identity is not the issue. Readers need only forget what they know about *how* the hero counters the villain in the story. Readers must be able to reimagine events from the hero's perspective.

LITERARY ANCESTORS AND DESCENDANTS OF THE THRILLER

Thrillers have deep literary roots. According to Palmer, "every major element in . . . [their] structure is borrowed." Even so, "the borrowed elements are welded together into something entirely new" (*Thrillers* 114). In the subsections below, we will examine each "borrowed element" and see how that element is transformed when it appears in its new context. We will also see that each borrowed element finds its way into John Grisham's novels.

The Heroic Romance

The hero of a thriller resembles a "medieval knight in shining armour, minus chastity, plus technology" (*Thrillers* 115). In both medieval romance (Palmer cites as an example the fourteenth-century Spanish story of Amadis of Gaul) and modern thriller, a hero acts out of morality and love, not in hopes of achieving a reward. In medieval times, even a heavenly reward was considered an inappropriate goal to aspire to, although heroes might properly hope to feel satisfaction for having done a good thing. Heroes of medieval literature often fought against class oppression "and the forces of an unjust social order" (122), whereas in the modern thriller class differences are less often the issue.

Certainly, Grisham's lawyers resemble medieval heroes because most of them act out of "morality and love," with few thinking first of rewards. Jake Brigance in *A Time to Kill*, Darby Shaw in *The Pelican Brief*, Reggie Love in *The Client*, Adam Hall in *The Chamber*, and Rudy Baylor in *The Rainmaker* all fight against class oppression and injustice, with the foremost thought in mind of doing the right thing. Only Mitch McDeere in *The Firm* ensures first that he will profit from his efforts to right a wrong. Otherwise, all Grisham's heroes come to recognize that doing right provides satisfaction that money won't buy.

The Gothic Novel

Thrillers are also indebted to Gothic novels, works set in medieval times and dependent for effect on ghosts, dark castles, and secret passages. From the Gothic novel, most notably Horace Walpole's *The Castle of Otranto* (published in 1765), thrillers have adopted a view of evil as the intrusion of massive disorder—signified by ghoulish elements—into an otherwise orderly world. The intrusion is so disruptive that it calls into question the order that has been interrupted. In Gothic literature "pathological irruption subverts the order of nature as a whole, whereas in the thriller it merely threatens the social order" (Palmer *Thrillers* 128).

All of Grisham's legal thrillers focus on massive disorder, often located where one would least expect to find it: within the legal/governmental system itself. Law in *A Time to Kill* treats black people different from whites. Mark Sway in *The Client* must hire Reggie Love to protect him from the juvenile justice system. By the end of *The Chamber* Adam Hall has decided to join the fight against capital punishment, which he feels is under any circumstance an unjust punishment for wrongdoing. Perhaps that legal thrillers locate evil where we most idealistically hope to find good is what gives them their special appeal.

Police Memoirs and Low-Life Literature

Thrillers owe two things to early crime literature such as *The Memoirs of Vidocq* (1828–1829), a classic French example of the form. First is the use of the detective, police officer, and, in legal thrillers, the lawyer as hero. Second is the way in which crime is presented: as the "exotic and threatening irruption" needed to achieve suspense (Palmer *Thrillers* 129).

Cowboy Fiction

Several critics see a connection between thrillers and western popular fiction. They relate the " 'mean streets,' male-dominated and dark [of hard-boiled detective thrillers], to the conventions of Western or 'cowboy' fiction of an earlier generation, showing us the transition between the rider of the purple sage who arrives to right the wrongs done to society by its outlaws and the 'private op' who, as vigilante, must do for society what it seems unable to do for itself" (Rader and Zettler xii). These critics also connect the hard-boiled detective to Natty Bumppo and other frontier heroes of American literature who worked alone and lived a solitary life (Baker and Nietzel 7).

As we shall see, Grisham's heroes are also loners in the cowboy tradition. Even Grisham's female lawyer heroes, Darby Shaw and Reggie Love, lead fairly solitary lives: Darby's lover dies early in *The Pelican Brief* and Reggie Love is bitterly divorced in *The Client*. Both work primarily alone, although someone helps them from time to time.

Besides literary ancestors, the thriller has literary descendants. There are "science-fiction private eyes, occult private eyes and religious private eyes" (Baker and Nietzel 11). These futuristic heroes are probably suggestive of things to come.

HISTORICAL BEGINNINGS OF THRILLERS IN AMERICA

Thrillers of all types in the United States, including legal thrillers, grew out of the public's interest in crime. In the mid-nineteenth century, urban Americans thought themselves to be in the middle of a crime wave, with danger lurking all around. Within a few decades, groups such as the New York Society for the Prevention of Crime began. One of the ways in which this group and others tried to control vice was by suppressing accounts of crime in local story papers, newspapers that published light fiction for large groups of readers: "200,000 and even 300,000 yearly subscribers were typical for the most popular publications" (Panek 9). One vice group worked to pass a law in Massachusetts prohibiting the sale of crime fiction to minors. Although they were somewhat successful in keeping police reports and crime studies out of print, they were unable to "suppress . . . vice or eradicate . . . crime" (8).

Meanwhile, police groups began creating histories of their work and releasing studies that "identified known criminals" (Panek 8). Police and detective memoirs appeared, and story papers (begun in the United States in the 1830s) grew even more popular than they had been. One type of material that became extremely popular was the Misery and Mystery story, a genre that resembled detective fiction. Misery and Mystery stories began in France and spread quickly to the United States. "This 'new' kind of fiction used the same old titillation romance motifs but replaced exotic settings with the sensational background of the corrupt city" (10). Dime novels, inexpensive fiction paperbacks, also became popular around this time; although dime novels were most often westerns, they also featured Misery and Mystery stories. Publishers, meanwhile, realized that readers were more interested in the exploits of a popular hero than in the name of the author who told the story. Therefore, efforts began to locate and develop writers who were interested in producing formulaic literary commodities instead of telling a story that was strictly of their own invention.

DETECTIVE FICTION

Detective novels with fictional detective heroes also became popular around this time. Panek believes that the "father" of American detective fiction, Edgar Allan Poe, was influenced by his years as a resident of Philadelphia and that Poe's experiences there played an important role in the development of the American detective or crime thriller. Because efforts to establish modern police forces in America began in Philadelphia, Poe was no doubt familiar with police history and police lore, some of which probably found their way into his "Murders in the Rue Morgue," "The Mystery of Marie Roget," and "The Purloined Letter" as well as into the characterization of his hero, the amateur detective Auguste Dupin (Panek 13). Poe's "detached amateur detective" disappeared in America for a few decades after "The Purloined Letter" was published in 1844 (13).

An official detective hero first appeared in American fiction in the mid-1860s:

> John B. Williams' *Leaves from the Notebook of a New York Detective* (1864–1865) contains 15 short stories about James Brampton, a New York private detective. Entering the world

of the story paper, *Beadle's Monthly* ran what is perhaps the first American detective novel, Seely Regester's (Mrs. Metta Victoria Fuller Victor) *The Dead Letter. The Saturday Journal* of June 10, 1871, ran *The Detective's Ward*; or *The Fortunes of a Bowery Girl* by 'Agille Penne' (Albert W. Aiken). George Munro's *The Fireside Companion*, however, seems to have played the most significant role in this initial attempt to es-tablish the detective as a popular hero." (Panek 14).

Frank Dumont's "My First Case" (June 27, 1868) was probably the first fully American detective story published in *The Fireside Companion*.

But American detective stories didn't become immediately popular thereafter. Not until *The Fireside Companion* ran the serial *Old Sleuth* did detective thrillers begin to catch on. Old Sleuth, the hero, was immensely popular, and more works by his creator, Tony Pastor (Harlan Page Halsey), quickly followed: *The Fastest Boy in New York, The Irish Detective*; or, *On His Track*, and *Down in a Coal Mine. The Fireside Companion* barely turned a profit in 1870; but with Old Sleuth in its pages, it had more than 250,000 subscribers by 1880 or so. One problem with early American detective fiction, according to Panek, was that much of it was set in small-town America. When detectives began solving crimes and catching criminals in big cities, detective stories developed a distinctly American flavor. Other problems with early American detective thrillers were un-developed detective heroes and sentimental plots. Once "writers under-stood that readers wanted to know about the hero as a detective and not as a participant in tear-jerking melodrama," the detective thriller became more popular, preparing the way for the popularity of the lawyer hero in legal thrillers (Panek 16).

Related to writers' discovery that readers wanted to know more about the detective hero was their realization that readers preferred stories about real-life detectives as opposed to fictional ones. Within certain de-tective series, several nonfiction works (including autobiographies by po-lice officials—sergeants, detectives, inspectors, captains, even retired officers) were supposedly published. It appears likely, however, that many of the stories promoted as biography and autobiography were actually fiction. Nevertheless, "real-life" detectives and "real-life cases" were what people wanted to read. This interest in real, not fictional, accounts of police work may persist to this day in readers' preference for legal fiction by lawyers. We are fascinated not by what could have happened but by what really did.

In the nineteenth century, where did this monumental interest in detective thrillers (preparing the way for contemporary interest in legal thrillers) come from? Probably from the way in which cities in the United States grew rapidly and changed. Although wealth increased in the new nation, until the 1820s a medieval system of "night watches" was all that protected the safety of urban populations. The cities of Philadelphia and New York began the nineteenth century with around 100,000 people apiece and ended it with populations of more than a million. As citizens grew wealthy, they vacated apartments above their shops to live in more pleasant districts, causing cities to develop clearly defined areas for shopping and industry that were largely unguarded at night. Also, the wealthier people became, the less inclined they were to join in neighborhood patrols, preferring instead to hire police officers to do the work they had formerly done themselves. Police departments—and, later, detectives—thus became essential to protecting the urban areas.

THE LEGAL THRILLER

"We hate lawyers, but we love stories about 'em," John Grisham observes. According to Jonathan Freedland, our fascination with courts, criminals, lawyers, and judges has its roots in American culture. Americans will sue anyone, even our parents. Our fascination for the law comes from the Constitution: it provides us with unbelievable rights. If one of us violates another's rights, that person is likely to expect redress (Freedland 2). And this fascination extends to what we read. Publishers used to believe that if they put a swastika on the cover of a paperback that was about to be published, the book would sell. Now a "somewhat tipped" scale of justice does the job. "The law has replaced Nazis as the fuel for commercial entertainment" (Streitfeld D1). Sydney Pollack, who directed the film version of *The Firm*, attributes Americans' considerable interest in legal thrillers to the cynicism and suspicion of the 1990s in which authority of any sort isn't to be trusted (*Current Biography* 221–224).

But readers may also find a more positive connection to legal fiction, in that stories venerating lawyers almost always end up affirming the system and the moral values the system represents. No matter how flawed or how "sleazy," the government almost invariably gets the job done in a Grisham novel. Unsurprisingly, Grisham—is the most popular writer of legal thrillers at more than one major District of Columbia bookstore. Because there are so many attorneys in Washington, there are always plenty looking for a good legal read. But more than just lawyers read Grisham.

Still, it's unsafe to conclude that legal thrillers are strictly a phenomenon of the 1990s, since interest in legal fiction—works that concern the efforts of a lawyer to obtain justice, usually in a courtroom—predates this decade. Just as late nineteenth-century American readers developed a fascination for detective thrillers, later readers saw the connection between the efforts of police and detectives to restore social order and those of lawyers to do the same thing. Melville Davisson Post was "this century's first important writer of stories about lawyers and the law" (Nevins 1). In a humanities course devoted to popular literature and the law offered through St. Louis University's School of Law, Nevins teaches four stories written by Post. One is "The Corpus Delicti" (1896), a piece depicting an attorney, Randolph Mason, who shows a client how to murder someone, admit in court to having done so, and get away with the deed. Other Post stories that are taught in the seminar include "The Life Tenant" (1907), in which Mason attains justice by using "the quirks and glitches in the legal system"; "The Tenth Commandment" (1912); and "Naboth's Vineyard" (1916). Susan Glaspell's "A Jury of Her Peers" (1917), canonized in dramatic form as *Trifles* in *The Norton Anthology of Literature by Women*, illustrates for Nevins's students "some of the motifs of feminist jurisprudence." A third early twentieth-century writer, Arthur Train, depicts "contradictory varieties of lawyering philosophy" in works such as "Mock Hen and Mock Turtle" (1919); "That Sort of Woman" (1921); "The Liberty of the Jail" (1922); "The Bloodhound" (1922); and "Mr. Tutt Is No Gentleman." "The Judge Laughed Last" by Dashiell Hammett, and Chapter 2 of S. S. Van Dine's *The Canary Murder Case*, deal with legal issues; the latter work contains "a self-standing Socratic dialogue on law, reason, and common sense" (1).

Examples of popular legal thrillers of the 1930s include Perry Mason novels by Earle Stanley Gardner. *The Case of the Howling Dog*, for example, reflects Depression-era attitudes toward the law. In Gardner's early works, Perry Mason is more of a "tiger in the . . . jungle" and less the idealized attorney we're familiar with from watching television (Nevins 3). William Faulkner's works, in particular "Smoke" (1935) and "Tomorrow" (1940), show that John Grisham's Oxford forebear in his treatment of legal themes is indebted to Melville Davisson Post. In the 1940s a popular theme in legal fiction and the culture was the need to occasionally take the law into one's own hands. Walter Van Tilburg

Clark's *The Ox-bow Incident* (1940) and Cornell Woolrich's "Three Kills for One" (1942) present vigilante justice, and Ellery Queen's *The Glass Village* (1954) illustrates the paranoia rampant during the Joseph McCarthy era. The best representative of late 1950s and early 1960s legal fiction is Harper Lee's *To Kill a Mockingbird* (1960), a novel reflective of the bigotry and ethnic struggles of the time. Louis Auchincloss's *Power in Trust* (1955) and John D. MacDonald's *The Executioners* (1958), which also dealt with legal issues, present an opposite view of the period. During the 1970s and 1980s there was a reaction in popular fiction against legal liberalism and "an ever-deepening disgust with lawyers and the legal system" (Nevins 3). Works from the 1970s such as Joseph Wambaugh's *The Blue Knight* (1973) and *The Onion Field* (1974) reflect these attitudes, as do Lawrence Block's "The Ehrengraf Method" (1977) and "The Ehrengraf Presumption" (1978). Legal conservatism continued in legal fiction of the 1980s. Geoffrey Norman's *Armed and Dangerous* makes "lawyers legally accountable for the clients they defend" (Nevins 3). Louis Auchincloss's "The Tender Offer" (1983), Tom Wolfe's *The Bonfire of the Vanities*, and Scott Turow's *Presumed Innocent* (1987) are cases in point.

Scott Turow deserves credit for the most recent popularity of the legal-thriller-by-lawyers genre. Turow, a former employee in the U.S. attorney's office in Chicago and more recently a lawyer in the Chicago firm of Sonnenschein, Nath & Rosenthal, was among the first attorneys to add the words "legal novelist" to their resumes. Turow explains his second profession as a writer by noting that all those years of "prosecuting corrupt lawyers and judges have given him a proctologist's view of . . . [his first] profession" (Torry WBIZ 5). Although attorneys had previously published nonfiction accounts of important cases and how-to texts involving legal issues, and although Louis Auchincloss was an attorney-turned-novelist, few had written fictional accounts focusing on legal situations. Turow's first legal thriller, *Presumed Innocent*, sold more than 700,000 hardcover copies and was on the *New York Times* best-seller list for hardcover fiction for 44 weeks.

Lawyers-turning-novelists are now a common occurrence, mostly because publishers regard works by attorneys as highly saleable. In an effort to cash in on the market, publishers promote these new writers as the next John Grisham or Scott Turow. It also helps to have lawyer-authors promoting their works in that they are experts at selling a case—whether in court, on a television talk show, or at a bookstore autograph session. Other lawyers, watching their colleagues turn a profit, then set to work on their own story. One agent reported having received in the last six months unsolicited proposals or manuscripts from 112 lawyers writing legal novels. Apparently all that fame, money, and glamour are appealing to lawyers. Unless they're F. Lee Baileys or Johnny Cochrans, most attorneys lead relatively boring, sometimes frustrating professional lives. When a colleague strikes it rich writing legal thrillers, others fantasize getting rich too. For example, Stanford University law professor Lia Matera has published two novels, *Where Lawyers Fear to Tread* and *Hidden Agenda*. She described her situation: "I looked at it as publish or practice" (Kaufman "Legions" A10). Publishing seemed to her the better choice. Other attorneys who have published legal thrillers in the last few years include Philip Friedman (*Reasonable Doubt*), Paul Levine (*Night Vision*), and James Duffy, a.k.a. Haughton Murphy (*Murder Takes a Partner*; *Murders and Acquisitions*). Also writing legal thrillers are:

William Bernhardt (*Double Jeopardy*)

Bill Blum (*Prejudicial Error*)

Jay Brandon (*Local Rules*)

William Coughlin (*Heart of Injustice*)

Alan Dershowitz (*The Advocate's Devil*)

William Diehl (*Show of Evil*)

Jonathan Harr (*A Civil Action Publisher*)

Clifford Irving (*Final Argument*)

D. Kincaid (*Lawyer's Tale*)

Joseph Klempner (*Felony Murder*)

Mimi Lavenda Latt (*Powers of Attorney*)

John T. Lescroart (*The Thirteenth Juror*)

Phillip Margolin (*The Last Innocent Man; After Dark*)

John Martel (*Conflicts of Interest*)

Steve Martini (*Undue Influence; Compelling Evidence; Prime Witness; The Simeon Chamber*)

Christine McGuire (*Until Justice Is Done*)

Arthur Nehrbass (*Dead Easy*)

Darien North (*Bone Deep*)

Perri O'Shaughnessey (*Motion to Suppress*)

Richard North Patterson (*Degree of Guilt*)

Barry Reed (*Indictment*)

Robert Robin (*Above the Law*)

Mary Taylor Rosenberg (*Trial by Fire*)

Lisa Scottoline (*Everywhere That Mary Went*)

Susan R. Sloan (*Guilt by Association*)

Grif Stockley (*Illegal Motion; Probable Cause*)

Robert Tannenbaum (*Justice Denied*)

Maynard Thomson (*Trade Secrets*)

Gallatin Warfield (*State v. Justice*)

William P. Wood (*Stay of Execution*)

Shelby Yastrow (*Under Oath*)

Even Joyce Carol Oates, although not a lawyer, has tried her hand at creating a legal thriller in her book *American Appetites*. A list this long reflects the view of David Gernert, former Vice President and editor-in-chief of the Editorial department at Doubleday, about how aware publishers are that legal thrillers, especially those written by lawyers, are extremely popular. Gernert mentions the "bandwagon factor." According to him, the more readers like legal thrillers—in particular, legal thrillers written by lawyers—the harder publishers will try to locate lawyers who are authors and the more they'll publish books by them (Fein D6). Why do readers hunger for legal fiction written by lawyers? For the thrill of knowing that an insider is telling the story, presenting details that give the novel an authentic feel.

But there is more to the appeal of legal-thrillers-by-lawyers than that the works put readers on the inside and in the know. Legal thrillers also offer readers resolution in the face of uncertainty, something real life rarely does. As for the lawyers themselves, there's probably a natural connection between practicing law and writing fiction. Words are lawyers' stock in trade. Lawyers must solve the kinds of puzzles that novelists deal with, so writing about lawyers doesn't constitute too big a stretch. Even the kind of organizing an attorney must do isn't all that different from what a writer does when putting together a novel. Scott Turow says that planning to present a case in court is much like figuring out how to narrate a novel. Courtroom witnesses are like narrators whom the lawyer must help in presenting their story to an audience (a jury) during a trial.

And lawyers have an added advantage over the nonlawyer writing about legal issues in that their practice is likely to have provided them with intriguing stories and characters. Grisham says that the lawyers he knows have great stories to tell about weird cases or crazy clients. Lawyers also have a touch of the psychologist in them. Over the years they deal with countless matters involving money and people, not to mention moral, ethical, and legal principles. They see how people behave in trying situations much as a psychologist does, and the skilled writers among them are able to present their analyses powerfully on paper.

GRISHAM AND THE LEGAL THRILLER

John Grisham's novels have been as successful as Scott Turow's. Although *The Firm* sold fewer hardcover copies (550,000) than did Turow's *Presumed Innocent*, Grisham distinguished himself in 1993 by having four novels at one time on the *New York Times* best-seller lists: *The Client* on the hardcover list; *The Firm*, *The Pelican Brief*, and *A Time to Kill* on the paperback list.

Grisham's and Turow's fictionalized view of the legal system hasn't been widely popularized for very long except on television. Although most Americans are familiar with television series focused on lawyers and court cases (for example, *Perry Mason* and *L. A. Law*), not until John Grisham and Scott Turow came along did we have a fictional parallel to television's ennobling and prettified take on the law. *L. A. Law*, in particular, glamorized the legal profession with its focus on corporate law and attractive lawyers. Grisham does the same thing. His characters have a corporate or civil practice, but they usually end up fighting for some legal or moral principle. If the film adaptations of Grisham's novels are any indication, his heroes are as glamorous as those on *L. A. Law*. Although Grisham claims he's interested in "average, ordinary people— with no training in espionage—forced to hit the road when somebody's trying to get them" (Conroy C1), that claim seems somewhat suspect. In at least four of his novels the average, ordinary people are lawyers—and gorgeous ones at that (played in the movies by the likes of Tom Cruise, Julia Roberts, and Susan Sarandon).

But Grisham's heroes aren't just good-looking crime fighters. Consistent with the thriller's format, Grisham pits a solitary, principled lawyer against a dark, looming force. Usually Grisham's heroes get involved unwittingly in a dangerous situation. He also makes sure the hero is sympathetic and that his or her life is at stake. Excitement depends on putting the lawyer in a life-threatening situation.

A *Los Angeles Times* article agrees and provides a tongue-in-cheek look at what the writer calls Grisham's *oeuvre*, the writer's claim being that Grisham has penned the same plot into each novel. Focusing on three Grisham novels and their film adaptations—*The Firm*, *The Pelican Brief*, and *The Client*—the *Times* film critic says of the Grisham hero that he/she is a "bright young man/woman" who is just starting out. Mitch in *The Firm* is embarking on a law career, Darby in *The Pelican Brief* is a law student, and Mark in *The Client* is a child who hires an idealistic lawyer who is relatively new to the profession. About the hero's problem, the *Times* claims that in:

> *The Firm*: "He [Mitch] knows something he shouldn't—that the Mafia runs his law firm."
>
> *The Pelican Brief*: "She [Darby] knows something she shouldn't—that a powerful oil billionaire paid for the killings of two Supreme Court justices."
>
> *The Client*: "He [Mark] knows something he shouldn't—where a Mafia thug buried a U.S. senator he murdered." (*Los Angeles Times* "First, Let's Top-Bill" 26).

Who is the villain in each of these works? In *The Firm*: corrupt lawyers and cruel hit men. In *The Pelican Brief*: an oil tycoon, corrupt lawyers, and cruel hit men. In *The Client*: cruel hit men.

In each novel the government (in the form of the FBI or U.S. attorney) asks the hero to put himself or herself at risk. In each novel the hero doesn't, for fear that the FBI won't be able to deliver on its promises. And in each novel the hero has unlikely allies who help. In the end, Mitch outsmarts both the Mafia and the FBI, Darby outsmarts both the billionaire and all the president's men, and Mark outsmarts both the Mafia and the U.S. attorney. Still, true to the negative thriller format, all is not roses for the hero. In *The Firm*, Mitch must leave the legal profession. In *The Pelican Brief*, Darby must abandon her law studies and hide. In *The Client*, Mark enters the witness protection program. Although *The Chamber* might be something of a break in this pattern, Grisham returns to it wholeheartedly in *The Rainmaker* with Rudy Baylor, another young attorney who by novel's end no longer wants to practice law, choosing instead to be a teacher.

GRISHAM, READERS, AND THE LAW

In "Law's Labors Lost: The Lawyer as Hero and Anti-Hero," Verlyn Klinkenborg captures John Grisham's (as well as the average American's) ambivalent feelings toward lawyers; she says we both denigrate and revere them. Klinkenborg adds that Americans define law loosely and largely as rules, the Constitution, and what we see when we watch *Perry Mason*, *Night Court*, *L.A. Law*, and *People's Court* on television. On one hand, we idolize lawyers as protectors of the democratic system; on the other, we despise lawyers and many of the trappings of the legal system. There is reason for our ambivalence. We sense how intricate and entangling the web of the law can be, and we realize that only lawyers feel comfortable "among those endlessly intersecting lines of force" that are brought to bear in a lawsuit against us (Klinkenborg 32). Another reason for our uncertainty about lawyers has to do with their too-frequent surrender to greed. Gone is the ideal of the lawyer/statesperson who strives to reconcile the facts of each case against the broader issues of public service. Greed, of course, has no place in such negotiations.

Although Klinkenborg labels John Grisham among the worst practitioners of the legal thriller, her arguments about Americans' ambivalence toward law are reflected in most, if not all, of Grisham's works. Although few of the issues Klinkenborg expects to be presented actually find their way into a Grisham novel—that is, we rarely see a lawyer struggling with his or her role as a lawyer/statesperson or asking what constitutes morality in a particular marketplace—all of Grisham's books depict the legal system and lawyers in their best and worst lights. The hero protagonist in each novel embodies the good that can come from law in a democracy, whereas the other lawyers in the novels often embody the larger obstructive legal environment against which the good lawyer struggles.

No one claims that popular culture is subtle. "While art dwells in ambiguity, popular culture thrives on extremes: good and evil, hero and villain, zealot and soothsayer" (Gillers 509). Grisham's novels underscore this point. A key moment in any legal thriller occurs when a district attorney defies the system, a public defender fights "the big boys in

plush offices who are perceived as bending the law to their own uses."
In these cases, the struggle occurs between "two visions of the law, the
one wealthy, corrupt, rotting from within, the other rotting from self-
hatred or vodka but essentially sound, still capable of having its ideals
aroused" (Klinkenborg 36). Although Grisham's Reggie Love may have
been a drinker, her recovery and self-esteem are intact at the beginning
of *The Client*. Adam Hall, Jake Brigance, Darby Shaw, and Rudy Baylor
are nearly to purely good and heroic. Mitch McDeere is tarnished, but
he is still "essentially sound," "still capable of having . . . [his] ideals
aroused" (Klinkenborg 36).

3

A Time to Kill
(1989)

A Time to Kill, Grisham's first novel, is his favorite. Set in fictional Ford County, Mississippi, the novel recounts the rape of a 10-year-old African-American girl and the efforts of a small-town lawyer, Jake Brigance, to defend the child's father after he murders the two white men who raped her. Grisham says his "motives were pure" when he wrote *A Time to Kill* (Mathews 79), by which he means he uncovered a story so powerful he felt he simply had to tell it. Early responses to Grisham's tale of legal revenge, however, might have indicated he alone felt the story's power. Numerous publishing houses and agents saw and rejected the novel before Jay Garon agreed to represent Grisham and before Wynwood Press bought the manuscript for $15,000. In time Wynwood did a first printing of 5,000 copies, at least a thousand of which Grisham himself bought. Not until Grisham's second novel, *The Firm*, became successful did people look with renewed interest at his first, which was eventually bought by Hollywood for a record-setting $6 million.

Grisham believes the power of *A Time to Kill* lies in its attention to detail. He claims it is better than his later novels in that readers can "smell the biscuits and the eggs and the grits and hear the chatter of the Coffee Shop." The novel's characters and setting are more realistic; readers can almost feel the "sweat sticking to their shirts in the July heat" (Mathews 79).

Although Grisham may be right that *A Time to Kill*'s power lies in part in its detailed portrayal of characters and setting, its power has another source: the novel's timeless plot. *A Time to Kill* tells about innocence defiled and about a confrontation between good and evil. Tonya Hailey is nearly killed by "two red-necks" whom Grisham makes clear have no socially redeeming value. Billy Ray Cobb and Pete Willard kidnap Tonya in Pete's yellow pickup truck, a confederate flag suspended in its back window. A macabre tailgate party ensues. Between beers and joints, the two men casually watch one another rape Tonya over and over again. After a time they don't even know whether their victim is alive or dead. They think she's alive because "niggers generally could not be killed by kicking and beating and raping" (2). Late in the afternoon they dump the child in a far corner of the county, leaving her for dead.

The rest of the novel focuses on the efforts of Carl Lee Hailey Jr., Tonya's father, to get revenge and on those of Jake Brigance, the county's sharpest lawyer, to defend Carl Lee for killing Cobb and Willard. Lining up with the forces for good are (besides Brigance) the town's black sheriff, Ozzie Walls; Jake's former partner, Lucien Wilbanks; Jake's attorney friend, Harry Rex Vonner; and a young law student from Ole Miss, Ellen Roark, who clerks for Jake. Besides Cobb and Willard, evil is represented by those in the justice system who would punish Carl Lee and those in town—most notably Ku Klux Klan members—who despise Carl Lee because he is black. Good and evil face off in and around the Ford County Courthouse during Carl Lee's trial, with most of the emphasis on courtroom action. Not until the last few pages do readers learn whether Jake will be able to get Carl Lee off. Readers also aren't told whether Jake Brigance's wife, Carla, and daughter, Hannah, who are threatened by white supremacist groups because Jake is defending a black man, will be safe.

PLOT DEVELOPMENT

Plot in fiction "is a plan or groundwork of human motivations, with the actions resulting from believable and realistic human responses. In a well-plotted work, nothing is irrelevant; everything is related" (Roberts and Jacobs 98). The plot of *A Time to Kill* shows a cause-and-effect relationship among three stories. The first concerns the kidnapping and rape of Tonya Hailey. The second details Carl Lee Hailey's plans to gain revenge by murdering his daughter's two attackers, and the third chronicles Carl Lee's defense mounted by attorney Jake Brigance. The first two stories make up most of the first seven chapters of the novel. The third story, that of Jake's defense of Carl Lee Hailey, comprises the novel's other 37 chapters.

The first part of *A Time to Kill* (Chapters 1 to 3) creates enough suspense to keep readers' attention throughout the rest of the novel. Grisham does not withhold the identity of Tonya's attackers; rather, he devotes Chapter 1 to describing the hideous crime, leaving readers to wonder whether justice will be achieved and the perpetrators punished. Having depicted the heinous activities of his antagonists at the beginning of *A Time to Kill*, in Chapter 3 Grisham introduces and begins to develop his protagonist, the lawyer Jake Brigance. The overriding question that propels the story line forward is: What role will Jake Brigance play in restoring order in Clanton and through a court of law? After all, readers immediately learn, Tonya's attackers do not hire Jake to defend them. Meanwhile, in part one Grisham heightens suspense by allowing readers to view Billy Ray and Pete's attack through Tonya's eyes, portraying the suffering of Tonya's mother when her daughter disappears, and detailing the moment when a weeping Carl Lee has to be forced to let go of his daughter in the ambulance on the way to the hospital. At the end of part one, Grisham lets readers sit in on Pete's confession.

In the novel's second part (Chapters 4 through 7), Grisham increases suspense once again through murder. Carl Lee shoots Billy Ray Cobb and Pete Willard with an M-16 as they are escorted between the courtroom and their jail cell; Grisham states their "skin and blood splashed together" (72). The murder does not occur in a vacuum. Grisham has Carl Lee discuss with Jake Brigance what he might do to his daughter's rapists, and he lets readers travel with Carl Lee to Memphis to secure a gun. Part of the novel's suspense grows out of readers' advance knowledge of Carl Lee's plans to murder Cobb and Willard. Then, too, having witnessed the murders, we wonder how justice can be served under the circumstances, since revenge does not constitute a legitimate defense plea.

In the third part of *A Time to Kill*, Jake Brigance defends Carl Lee in a fascinating trial. Because readers know Carl Lee is guilty of committing the murders, Grisham maintains suspense by leaving readers to wonder whether Carl Lee will be found guilty of murdering Cobb and Willard and by gradually revealing Jake Brigance's courtroom strategies for saving Carl Lee's life. Other events in the novel that are used to increase suspense include death threats on Jake and his family, an assault on Ellen Roark, and the impending danger of Ku Klux Klan intervention.

Each of *A Time to Kill*'s 44 chapters contains several short episodes that give the novel its fast pace. Episodes usually focus on the activities of one character. Often Grisham begins the episode with that character's name and a reference to the date or time of day in which the action occurs. This structuring technique lets readers feel as if they are being escorted by a knowledgeable narrator, one who keeps them up on the late-breaking news pertaining to the case. Since the narrator reports on the feelings of characters as well as their activities, and since the narrator seems to know especially well the thoughts of the novel's protagonist, Jake Brigance, readers tend to trust that voice and allow themselves to be caught up in the action. The occasional slip-up (such as when the narrator says Judge Percy Bullard asks his deputy, Mr. Pate, to bring him a second Styrofoam cup of ice water, their code phrase for vodka, into the courtroom when a first hasn't been delivered) isn't enough to deter that trust (68). Events seem real and readers have a front-row seat for the action.

CHARACTER DEVELOPMENT

A common criticism about Grisham's writing is that characterization—"the creation of imaginary persons so that they seem lifelike" (Holman and Harmon 80)—takes a back seat to plot. If this generalization is true in *A Time to Kill*, it is less so than in his other works. Clearly, Grisham likes Jake Brigance and wants readers to like him too, so he devotes considerable attention to creating his fictional, loner attorney. There's probably a reason for Grisham's affection for Jake. In an "Author's Note" to the novel, he admits:

> There's a lot of autobiography in this book. I no longer prac-
> tice law, but for ten years I did so in a manner very similar
> to Jake Brigance. I represented the people, never banks or in-
> surance companies or big corporations. I was a street lawyer.
> Jake and I are the same age. I played quarterback in high
> school, though not very well. Much of what he says and does
> is what I think I would say and do under the circumstances.
> We both drive Saabs. We've both felt the unbearable pressure
> of murder trials, which is something I try to capture in the
> story. We've both lost sleep over clients and vomited in court-
> house rest rooms. (xi–xii)

In fact, readers can also see in Jake Brigance a more fully developed model of Grisham's other protagonists. There are elements of Jake in Mitch McDeere (*The Firm*), Darby Shaw (*The Pelican Brief*), Reggie Love (*The Client*), Adam Hall (*The Chamber*), and Rudy Baylor (*The Rainmaker*). All his heroes share Grisham's ambivalence toward the law. All eventually get to places Grisham has been in: they prefer to represent the common person in trouble, or they choose to leave their legal careers behind. All of them learn or already know that big business and big government are corrupt. They are romantics who see themselves as champions of the underdog, as principled practitioners within the justice system or as outcasts because the system itself is flawed.

Although Jake is more fully developed than any other Grisham hero, he is still something of a stereotype. As Grisham presents him, Jake embodies forces of reason and principle. He champions what's "good"— those who would avenge the rape of Tonya Hailey—against the "evil" perpetrators and the Neanderthals in Ford County, in particular the Ku Klux Klan, who might secretly excuse the rape of a black child. Jake's introduction in Chapter 3 casts him as a clear thinker, as one who "had a way of cutting through the excess and discussing the meat of any issue," a quality others in town appreciate. He lives by self-created rules, has an adoring wife and daughter, and hones a sense of humor that requires he "say smart things to the waitresses." He's the kind of person who owns a mutt rather than a particular breed of dog. He is one of the few professionals welcome at Clanton's local Coffee Shop, where he is "accepted by the blue collars, most of whom at one time or another had found their way to his office for a will, a deed, a divorce, a defense, or any one of a thousand other problems" (22). That readers are privy to more of Jake's thoughts than those of any other character encourages our identification with him.

Other less central characters are more two-dimensional and embody good along with Jake. Ozzie Walls, the only African-American sheriff in Mississippi, is an athlete and longtime friend of Jake's. They played football against each other during high school, and the two continue to razz one another about a particularly grueling game during which Ozzie broke Jake's leg. Readers trust Ozzie in part because Jake does, but also because he manages to be reelected sheriff in a county that is 74 percent white. Ozzie's honest responses to Jake's questions about being black also show him to be a force for good in the community.

Jake's former law partner, Lucien Wilbanks, despite deep character flaws, also represents the forces of good. Liberal in a conservative com-

munity, moneyed, alcoholic, and consummately cynical, Lucien was dis-
barred after appearing drunk at a strike and being convicted of assault
and battery and drunk and disorderly conduct. Although Lucien turned
his practice over to Jake after his disbarment, he continues to mentor his
friend. Because he fears no one and wants for nothing, his advice is
generally sound.

Jake's other associate, Ellen Roark, also ranks among the forces of
good. She shows up conveniently a little more than halfway through the
novel, after Carla leaves town with Hannah. Ellen, a law student at Ole
Miss, helps Jake put together Carl Lee's defense. She prepares short
briefs, types 90 words a minute, and researches evidentiary points. Besides providing support for Jake, she affords sexual tension in the novel.
She is obviously someone whom Jake finds attractive. She combines the
best of the two worlds—professional and personal—Jake generally keeps
separate. Ellen is smart, drives a black BMW, likes to talk law, mixes a
mean margarita, enjoys hanging out with Harry Rex and Jake, mocks
her "sweet little sorority girl" mother, wears starched jeans, and (like
the author who created her) resists wearing socks with her loafers. Qualified as a colleague, Ellen nevertheless knows her place as a woman in
Jake's world. She promises Jake she will work for free, carry his briefcase,
and make him coffee. Under her professional-looking, oversized, button-
down white shirts, she wears no bra.

In Grisham's view, Carl Lee and his brother Lester also operate on the
side of good. Billy Ray Cobb and Pete Willard deserve to die for what
they have done, and Carl Lee is a suitable avenging angel. Carl Lee is a
war hero, a dutiful husband and father, a loyal friend and brother. After
killing Billy Ray and Pete, he tells Jake how sorry he feels for their
"mommas and daddies." Lester Hailey returns home from Chicago the
moment he's told of the attack on his niece. He stays at his brother's side
throughout the rest of the novel.

On the other side of the equation are the two-dimensional forces of
evil, embodied by Billy Ray Cobb and Pete Willard. Billy Ray, at age 23,
has already been locked up in the penitentiary at Parchman. Grisham
characterizes him as a "tough little punk" who sells drugs. He is so cruel
he slings a half-empty beer can at Tonya between rapes and laughs when
the foam rolls off her stomach. Hanging out in a bar before his arrest,
Billy Ray tells those assembled he's finally "found a nigger who's a virgin" (15). When someone asks how old she is, Cobb answers "eight or
nine." Pete Willard is no finer a fellow. A little older than Billy Ray and
not as smart, he does whatever his friend and employer tells him to do.

But the forces of evil go beyond Tonya's attackers. Most of the judicial system in Ford County is pocked by those who use it for their own gain or self aggrandizement. A judge sits drunk in court. A county prosecutor uses his position to heighten his sense of self-importance. The towns-people, including members of the Ku Klux Klan who make death threats against Brigance, also constitute the forces he must combat. These people become instantly silent when Marshall Prather, while sitting in the Coffee Shop, asks Jake if he defended Billy Ray a couple years ago.

Grisham, like any writer, had three ways in which to develop his char-acters: by telling readers who they are and how they think; by showing the characters in action; or by presenting the characters from the inside, letting readers see how they think and what they value (Holman and Harmon 80). Like many popular writers, Grisham relies on the second of these devices with a little direct exposition thrown in to sharpen the outline of important characters like Jake.

SOCIAL/HISTORICAL CONTEXTS

The two issues that place *A Time to Kill* in social/historical context are racism and sexism. More than one hundred years after the Civil War, and despite the civil rights movement of the 1960s, African Americans continue to feel the effects of slavery. Women, too, remain second-class citizens, despite a resurgence of the women's movement during the 1970s. In fact, many women who worked in the civil rights movement of the 1960s were the same ones who struggled to achieve sexual equality in the 1970s. These women realized while serving coffee to male liberals, both black and white, as they championed equal rights for African Amer-icans, that females in America also suffer the indignities of inequality. Although the women's movement occurred throughout the country, the struggle for black rights took place predominantly in the southern United States.

Thus, Grisham's assertion that his novels could be set anywhere is untrue for *A Time to Kill*. Although Grisham may not be as preoccupied with place as were William Faulkner and another Mississippi writer, Eudora Welty, information about ethnic tension in fictional Ford County helps heighten suspense and makes readers realize that justice, in the case of Carl Lee Hailey, may not be achieved. The novel's social/histor-ical material also helps explain why Carl Lee takes the law into his own

hands instead of waiting for the legal system to creak its way to a conclusion.

Grisham implies that the justice system in Ford County is and always
has been white. The streets surrounding the courthouse, the seat of that
system, are named after presidents Adams, Washington, and Jefferson;
the names of Lincoln and Grant are noticeably absent. The courthouse
sits "quite naturally" in a square at the center of town, placed there by
the town's founding father, General Clanton (21). Even the position of
the courthouse suggests white supremacy in that it was rebuilt after Yan-
kees burned the first one down: it "defiantly faces south as if telling
those from the North to politely and eternally kiss its ass" (21). The
courthouse and the columns that support it are white. Every four years
a southern tradition is renewed when the Boy Scouts apply a new coat
of sticky white paint.

Grisham's novel reminds us that the law hasn't accorded African
Americans equal justice. For years, whites killed blacks and few cared;
in some cases, black people were even shot for sport. Lynchings were
commonplace for blacks who dared to fight back. Early on in *A Time to
Kill*, Grisham makes clear that things have not radically changed in contemporary Ford County. Many in the community resent having two
white men arrested for raping a little black girl. They seem not to understand that a crime has been committed. Further, they resent Jake Brigance, a white attorney, for defending a black man who killed the rapists,
even though Jake has without reprisal defended blacks for killing blacks.
When Billy Ray Cobb and Pete Willard get locked up, Clanton's jail is
populated solely by blacks.

In *A Time to Kill*, Grisham gives readers a thumbnail sketch of racial
issues and the civil rights movement of the 1960s. Ozzie, the town's black
sheriff, graduated in the late 1960s in the first mixed class at the local
high school. He wanted to go to college at Ole Miss and be on the football team, but he couldn't because the team already had two blacks on
it—a reminder of ethnic quotas in use at the time.

Curiously, Grisham champions the plight of African Americans, but
his narrative voice and male characters seem insensitive to women. In *A
Time to Kill* the female characters are negatively stereotyped as somewhat
crazy, unpleasant, or dangerously sexual. From the beginning of the
novel, Gwen Hailey is characterized (even by her husband) as unreasonable, hysterical even. When she becomes worried that Tonya has not
returned home from an errand, she calls her husband at the mill where
he works. Carl Lee does not come right home from work because Gwen

has called him several times in the past—unnecessarily, he thinks—when she was worried about her children's safety. Although Carl Lee's sons are equally anxious about Tonya's well-being, they are described by Carl Lee as "scared to death" (46). Carl Lee describes Gwen, on the other hand, as being "crazy" (46) or "crazier than normal" (49). Carl Lee's reaction to Gwen's behavior is interesting in that he is the one who is so driven by his pain that he kills the two men who are accused of raping his daughter.

Jake, like Carl Lee, thinks his wife is unreasonable when she questions his authority in a family crisis. During a bomb scare at the Brigance home, Jake hollers to Carla to get the keys to the car and take Hannah away from the house without ever explaining why. When Carla asks why, he yells back at her to just do as he says. When Carla demands again to know what's going on, Jake snaps that he'll tell her later and that she's to stay away from the house for 30 minutes. Not until Carla demands for the third time to know why Jake is yelling at her and telling her to drive away does Jake tell Carla there's dynamite close by. Although Jake doesn't specifically say Carla is hysterical, he implies that her reluctance to obey him is unreasonable. Jake's treatment of Carla comes as no surprise, considering his description of an ideal wife: such a woman stays at home, is beautiful, has babies, and doesn't try to wear the pants (286).

Ethel Twitty, the firm's loyal secretary for 41 years, is described as unpleasant and incompetent. She disobeys Jake's cardinal rule—she lets someone into Jake's office without his being there. When Jake returns and finds that someone has invaded his sacred territory, he berates Ethel, venting his long-standing frustration with her. One by one, Jake lists all the things he hates about Ethel including her attitude, voice, insubordination, and treatment of others. When Ethel tries to explain her action, Jake comes to within inches of her face and threatens to fire her if she doesn't do exactly what he tells her to do. Jake's discourteous response to Ethel is similar to his treatment of Carla; it is arrogant and shows that Jake has the greater power.

All the men, even "good" ones, treat women badly in *A Time to Kill*. The most obvious abuse of females is, of course, the raping of Tonya Hailey. But the rape is part of a larger pattern. Billy Ray and Pete, prior to raping Tonya, were at a lake with a friend and some women who were supposed to be loose but proved "untouchable" (4). Though Cobb provides plenty of alcohol and dope to the women, the women don't reciprocate his generosity. Frustrated at being rebuffed, the two men drive around aimlessly until they happen upon another female, though a young one, Tonya Hailey. Willard knocks the child unconscious by hitting her in the back of the head with a beer can. Clearly, the two men's behavior reflects their assumption that if one female doesn't accede to their wishes, another can be made to.

K. T. Bruster, a friend of Carl Lee's from Vietnam days, now owns a string of strip joints for blacks in Memphis. Though his career began modestly with the purchase of a small bar bought with the proceeds from a couple of pounds of hashish brought back from the war and a prostitute won in a poker game with a pimp, he prospers now (55). The marquees above "Cat's" joints unabashedly advertise beer and breast, but everyone knows more can be bought.

Another example of males on the side of "good" mistreating females comes at the hands of Lucien, Lucien's father, and Dr. W. T. Bass. Lucien, like his father, has a penchant for young, underaged females. Both have sex with females under the age of statutory consent; but they justify their actions by living with, financially supporting, or marrying at least one of them. Lucien, who admits to being drunk and "chasing little native girls" on the Cayman Islands, provides Sallie, a young black Caribbean woman (she's described as being under 30 years old but is so under that age that Jake asks Lucien how old she is) with a job and a place to live; his father, also a lawyer, financially supported Ethel Twitty (then his 17-year-old secretary), who bore his illegitimate children; and Dr. W. T. Bass marries the 17-year-old he's feloniously convicted of raping (31).

Even Harry Rex and Jake speak badly of Ellen Roark, hiding their malicious views behind a veneer of benign male banter. While joking about Ellen Roark, Harry Rex asks Jake if he's had sex with Ellen. Jake quickly responds that he hasn't slept with her because, after all, he's not crazy. Harry Rex accuses Jake of being crazy because he *hasn't* had sex with her and confidently announces that Jake's new law clerk can be "had" (371). Jake responds that he already has enough on his mind and tells Harry Rex to go for it.

Jake defers blame for his prurient interest in Ellen onto the object of his desire—Ellen herself. Jake is delighted when Ellen shows up unexpectedly (and braless) at his office. She personifies his pressureless days of law school when he drank lots of beer and dated often. Though Jake likes being married and misses his wife, he longs for a break from the pressures of Carl Lee's case. He misses drinking with friends, debating legal theories, and being free of debt. Ellen represents all those vestiges of freedom; she drinks a lot, is second in her class, and offers to work for free because she's already rich. Smitten by his young, beautiful, and articulate law clerk, Jake gives Ellen a key to his office. Ellen is allowed free reign in an area where no one in the world—not even Jake's wife—has been allowed.

To conceal his interest in Ellen, Jake accuses her of being sexually interested in him. One night while watching television coverage of their case on the news, Ellen asks Jake if he misses his wife. Jake suggestively replies that he misses his wife in more ways than Ellen can imagine. On another occasion while Jake and Ellen are on their way to a restaurant far enough away that no one will know them, out of the blue Jake announces to Ellen that the dinner is strictly business. When Ellen says she knows the dinner is business-only, Jake insists he knows what Ellen's really thinking and that she's got sex on her liberated mind. Ellen accuses Jake of having the ideas, but he denies the accusation. He reasserts that she's the one with the ideas (353). Finally, Jake's most blatant deferment of blame happens one evening when he rehearses in front of Ellen his opening statements for Carl Lee Hailey's trial. After two hours of practice, many interruptions by Ellen, and a few rounds of drinks, Jake's speech is perfect (396). After fetching another round of margaritas, Jake and Ellen go out on the balcony outside his office to watch the candlelight vigil in the square below. Ellen, who has been accused many times by Jake of wanting to be intimate with him, begins massaging Jake's neck. As he relaxes, she presses against him and rubs his shoulders. Jake says he's tired and asks Ellen where she's going to sleep for the night. Ellen answers his question by asking a question; she wants to know where he wants her to sleep. When he tells her she should sleep back at her college apartment, she asks him where he intends to sleep. Suddenly sanctimonious, Jake replies that he's going to spend the night in the house that he and *his wife* own. Through this maneuver Jake successfully baits the hook to catch Ellen, then blames Ellen for biting it.

Although Grisham's depiction in *A Time to Kill* of male-female relations is curious, it is not surprising. Jake Brigance's treatment of Ellen Roark is realistically portrayed. Like Jake and his male friends, many men resist dealing with their deeply held fear of intimacy with women and with their bad behavior where women are involved.

THEMATIC ISSUES

As with all Grisham novels, a central theme of *A Time to Kill* is that even though the search for justice may propel the actions of a few people, some of whom are lawyers, it must overcome obstacles within the legal system itself. Without the efforts of a Jake Brigance, Carl Lee Hailey would today be dead or languishing in the fictional Parchman penitentiary. Grisham's distrust of the legal system coincides with current popular attitudes toward the law: the famous trials of our time—those of William Kennedy Smith, O. J. Simpson, the Menendez brothers, for example—lead many people to question the effectiveness or at least the efficiency of our legal system.

Despite his own lack of faith in the legal system, Grisham in *A Time to Kill* affirms the individual's ability to untangle moral, ethical, and legal issues. Jake Brigance must do so to defend Carl Lee Hailey against murder charges. Carl Lee does the same thing before deciding to kill his daughter's rapists. There is historical precedence for the two men's faith. In his Nobel Prize acceptance speech (delivered in Stockholm on December 10, 1950), William Faulkner referred to "the old verities and truths of the heart, the old universal truths lacking which any story is ephemeral and doomed—love and honor and pity and pride and compassion and sacrifice," and he expressed faith that humankind "will prevail." Although Grisham refers to himself as one who "sells" books, not as an "artist" expressing eternal verities, through his creation of Carl Lee Hailey and Jake Brigance he comes close to affirming the views Faulkner expressed in Stockholm. Rightly or wrongly, Carl Lee shoots his daughter's rapists as a matter of honor; and Jake Brigance, understanding that honor is the issue, defends the killer.

A further thematic connection between Faulkner, other southern writers, and Grisham involves their awareness that the past continues to assert itself on the present. Throughout *A Time to Kill*, the old racist ways and attitudes linger. Even Ozzie, the black sheriff, uses the word "nigger" when eliciting a confession from Pete Willard. "Nigger" litters conversations in the novel, even though many who use the term know when to substitute the word "black." Grisham metaphorically suggests that new and old ways coexist in Clanton when he situates Jake Brigance's office on the north side of the courthouse square whereas the Sullivan law firm, which represents the moneyed Old South, occupies the square's southwest corner. Jake detests the Sullivan firm because it is comprised of "pompous and arrogant jerks" (27).

A fourth theme is that outsiderism—appearing aloof from or ambivalent toward the system—is the only way to maintain one's values and integrity. Although Jake sees himself as an outsider, he is certainly not an outsider of the Dirty Harry or Mad Max variety; that is, his rebellion takes place safely within the system. A lawyer, he is well liked by neighbors, co-workers, and friends in his home town. Jake has had a law partner, although he now practices alone because "there was no other lawyer in Clanton competent enough to practice with him" (27). Even the home he lives in shows his ambivalence. He shares a Victorian house with his wife and daughter, one of only two homes in Ford County that are on the National Register of Historic Places. Such a house might seem to embody the Old South, complete with columns in the front, but it is painted in contemporary colors—blue, teal, peach, and white—selected by a paint consultant from New Orleans. Despite his decision to remain close to his southern roots, Jake drives the only Saab (a red one) in Ford County.

Grisham romantically believes that outsiderism enables Jake to understand Carl Lee's need for revenge and helps Jake mount Carl Lee's defense. Still, Jake's position as outsider may place him too close to the edge. At the end of *A Time to Kill*, Jake has decided to leave Clanton. He may even quit his law practice—as Grisham has, and as have his protagonists Mitch McDeere in *The Firm* and Rudy Baylor in *The Rainmaker*.

A fifth theme relates to outsiderism and centers around Carl Lee's act of revenge. Grisham apparently sees taking the law into one's hands as a praiseworthy act, one for which the perpetrator ought not be punished. Tied to the American frontier is the notion that there is valor in doing the work of the law when the law isn't there. Although Jake himself doesn't step outside the bounds of law, he understands Carl Lee's decision to do so and is prepared to defend him for his actions.

AN EXISTENTIAL READING OF *A TIME TO KILL*

Much of modern literature assumes an existential view of the world. Existentialists believe that humans face life alone and are forced to make decisions even though there is no objective, rational, moral frame for doing so. Like Soren Kierkegaard, an important early existentialist philosopher, existentialists believe they must decide what is true, realizing "truth" is something others may define differently from the way they do. With Friedrich Nietzsche, another early proponent of existentialism, existentialists believe that each person must choose which situations should be defined as "moral" ones. All existentialists emphasize the importance of acting with certainty despite the uncertainty of the modern world. We come closest to the truth, they believe, when we are actively involved in the process of living.

Existentialists believe in choice rather than predestination. They would say that we are not fixed by biology or destiny. Along with that freedom to choose, however, is the inescapability of having to make choices. When we refuse to make a choice, we actually *have* chosen in that we allow a set of circumstances to occur. Thus, choice involves being committed to decisions we have made and taking responsibility for our actions. In honoring one's choices, Kierkegaard believed, a person must be prepared to defy the values and norms of the society in which one lives.

Dread accompanies choice in an irrational world. This is no surprise, since regardless of the choice a person makes, there is no possibility of having that choice externally validated as moral or right. Besides experiencing dread at making individual decisions, individuals feel a generalized anxiety at having constant freedom to make choices.

The view that the world is irrational and incomprehensible is important to existential thinking. "For existentialists, society has overvalued rationality and technology at the expense of losing from consciousness a fundamental sense of 'authentic' being; individuals thus live in a world that has no more than an absurd, superficial meaning and that threatens to devolve into nothingness" (Childers and Hentzi 103). We do not know why we are here. Lacking any clear path through the world, the existentialist defines a goal and follows it passionately, aware that death is the only ending to one's labors and that life is ultimately meaningless. Some existentialists, such as Blaise Pascal and Soren Kierkegaard, emphasize the paradoxical and even humorous elements of human existence in such a world. Others, in particular Jean-Paul Sartre, regard the human situation pessimistically. They believe that lacking a rational basis for our actions, humans are doomed to futile if passionate lives.

Existentialism has held as vital a place in literary studies as it has in philosophy. Famous literary works from the late nineteenth century to the present develop existential themes. One of the first to do so, Fyodor Dostoyevsky's *Notes from the Underground*, features an alienated hero who can no longer trust the claims of rationalism. Franz Kafka's *The Trial* and *The Castle*, André Malraux's *Man's Fate*, Albert Camus's *The Stranger*, Jean-Paul Sartre's *Nausea*, James Joyce's *Ulysses*, and Virginia Woolf's *To the Lighthouse* and *Mrs. Dalloway* are modern European novels that develop existentialist themes. Sartre's *Nausea* compellingly describes an individual's physical response (nausea) to realizing how irrational the world is. Among American writers, the modernist Ernest Hemingway is probably best known for his existential novels and stories. In *The Old Man and the Sea*, an elderly man named Santiago embodies an existentialist ethic. In fact, all of Hemingway's heroes, from Jake Barnes in *The Sun Also Rises* onward, fit somewhere on an existentialist continuum. Labeled ''code heroes'' by critics, these protagonists place themselves squarely midstream—in war, in the bullring, on a fishing boat—and struggle passionately to achieve goals, knowing that death is always waiting downstream. Other American writers whose works contain notably existentialist themes include Walker Percy, John Updike, John Barth, Norman Mailer, and Arthur Miller.

Jake Brigance in *A Time to Kill* is a popular fiction version of an existentialist hero. A seeker of truth who pursues his goals, Jake shares his first name with Hemingway's existential hero, Jake Barnes. Like other existentialist heroes, Jake Brigance seeks truth alone. His status as loner, however, seems somewhat selfishly motivated. Although Jake has family and colleagues from whom he elicits favors, we rarely see Jake return what he takes. Even Jake's parents do not receive much attention from their son. Involved in a high-profile case, Jake doesn't stay in touch, leaving Carla instead to maintain family ties. He keeps even more distant from his in-laws but assumes they will be glad to protect Carla and daughter Hannah when their safety is at risk. From Carla, Jake takes all the comfort he can: a beautiful home, daughter, and bountiful comforts. What Carla gets in return is enough articles in newspapers to create a scrapbook about Jake. His relationships with colleagues, although cordial, also reflect distance and one-sidedness. From Ozzie, for example, Jake gets the promise that Carl Lee will be given good care while in jail. Harry Rex basks and drinks in Jake's reflected glow.

Certainly, the world Jake inhabits—Clanton, Mississippi—is chaotic in the existentialist sense. There is nothing sane about a world in which two drunken men kidnap, torture, and rape a girl because she is young and black. There is nothing rational or objective about a judicial system that sentences each man to life plus 20 years (life for rape and 10 years apiece for kidnapping and assault) but allows him to be paroled in 13 years. There is nothing moral about a system that would probably sentence Carl Lee to the gas chamber because he is black and has killed two white men, but might protect a white man if the circumstances were reversed.

In that world Jake must make choices, and no sooner does he take Carl Lee's case than he begins receiving death threats. His house is burned by those who believe a black man does not deserve a fair trial. In Clanton the rules of the Old South still operate, and Jake challenges those rules. The Ku Klux Klan metaphorically represents the worst of old southern values.

The legal system is also part of the chaotic world within which Jake operates. Jake knows that for many in local government the reelection of county officials is more important than justice. Jake knows that Judge Percy Bullard will automatically bind Carl Lee over to a Grand Jury to avoid having to make an unpopular decision that might cost him votes. The ultimate in chaos is Judge Bullard's drinking vodka while presiding over Carl Lee's hearing.

The "truth" Jake seeks is complicated: Should Carl Lee Hailey be punished for his crime? Carl Lee has committed two premeditated slayings and, in the process, has shot a peace officer. What about the unwritten law of the South that states a black person who kills a white deserves an especially ugly fate? Jake, who seeks an acquittal for Hailey, has to override all his beliefs shaped by the law, feeling as he does that Carl Lee's retribution for his daughter's rape is justified. Jake must make other ethical decisions as well. Though Jake wants to defend Carl Lee and is disappointed when at one point in the case Carl Lee fires him, Jake refuses to compromise when asked by Bo Marsharfsky to be local Mississippi counsel. Jake won't associate his name with that of a man whose reputation has come from defending gangsters, thieves, and pimps and who solicits clients, an act that is a felony in Mississippi.

Although Jake seeks validation for his decision to defend Carl Lee, he doesn't get it from his mentor and former law partner, Lucien Wilbanks. Lucien (his name resembling that of the devil, Lucifer) is too cynical to care as deeply as Jake about Carl Lee's fate or to apply the laws rationally. When Jake questions Lucien about the possibility of an insanity defense, Lucien justifies his support for such a defense because he knows that vigilante justice will not be tolerated and that a jury needs justification for being sympathetic rather than legally right.

During a visit with Lucien, Jake feels his confidence shift to dread. Before the visit, Jake exudes positive vibrations about the case and reflects this confidence in a press conference. That he is even willing to talk to the press—a group that Grisham characterizes as particularly unpredictable—is itself a sign of confidence. At Lucien's home, however, Jake's positive feelings are undermined as Lucien methodically and playfully pokes holes in Jake's logic. After talking with Lucien, Jake walks to the edge of the porch and leans against a column. He feels weak. What is sport to Lucien is harmful to Jake in that it underscores the irrationality of the world in which Jake practices law.

The Firm
(1991)

The Firm, Grisham's blockbuster second legal thriller, was the best-selling novel of 1991 in the United States. Based on an idea that occurred to him in law school while watching big firms recruit top students, Grisham details in *The Firm* what could happen if one such law firm were owned by an organized crime mob. According to Grisham, in law school the students talked a lot about the salaries and benefits big firms were offering and how job applicants never really knew a company, what work that company did, or who it represented until the applicants were offered a job and accepted employment ("Author Likes" 5D). Some friends of his interviewed with a big firm in Dallas and came home wondering whether the firm might deal with underworld clients. Unassuming, Grisham notes that he never dreamed he would write a book on the topic, but for some reason the idea stayed with him (Will F1).

Grisham's hero in *The Firm* is Mitch McDeere, a Harvard Law School graduate ranked third in his class who is innocently lured into employment by Bendini, Lambert & Locke of Memphis, Tennessee—a company McDeere later learns is owned by the Morolto crime family from Chicago. That McDeere joins the firm is unsurprising since he is $23,000 in debt from law school and drives a Mazda hatchback that he has to roll downhill to start. Bendini, Lambert & Locke offers him a base salary of $80,000 the first year with a $5,000 raise when he passes the bar exam, not to mention a $90,000 income guaranteed the second year, bonuses, a low-interest home mortgage, a pay-off of his school loans, two country club memberships, plenty of help passing the bar exam, and a brand new BMW.

Because the law firm is the focus of an FBI sting operation, McDeere, at first unaware of the firm's illegal money-laundering schemes, soon gets caught between a proverbial rock and two hard places. The FBI wants Mitch to gather evidence against his employers, whose nefarious activities they have been tracking. But doing so would lead to ruin. If McDeere helped the FBI collect evidence against the firm, he would ruin his career as a lawyer and spend the rest of his life at the mercy of the government in a victim/witness protection program. A second option would be to do nothing; but if Mitch continued working for the firm, he would sooner or later commit illegal acts and be subject to arrest when the FBI closed in. A third possibility would be to get out of his contract with Bendini, Lambert & Locke; but if he did so, he would likely end up dead—five other associates of the firm have died in recent years under mysterious circumstances.

Grisham flagrantly concedes having written the novel to make money. He began it the day after finishing *A Time to Kill* and finished it two months after *A Time to Kill*'s publication. To his surprise, film rights to *The Firm* were bought for $600,000 before he had even found the manuscript a publisher. Hollywood's purchase of the book brought the project to the attention of publishers in New York, and before long a competition to publish Grisham's novel began. Doubleday emerged victorious from the fray.

Although reviewers agree the novel is a potboiler, a work written for money, many commented that it contained interesting information and that they couldn't stop turning its pages. The *San Francisco Chronicle* called it "an old-fashioned battle between the good guys and the bad guys" (Selvin E5). The *Houston Post* labeled it "clever" and "action-packed," adding that it "makes the world of law and high finance clear to the average reader" (Lee C5). A reviewer in *Cosmopolitan* commented that her boyfriend "stood on his head to get my attention, but I couldn't tear myself away from the last chapter of *The Firm* long enough to notice. When I was finally done, he grabbed the book and disappeared for hours. A rare accord" (Bernikow 40). *Newsweek* cataloged some of the "useful information" the novel contains, such as "how to send the massed troops of justice in the wrong direction, and how to move dirty money among numbered accounts" (Prescott 63). Even comedian Billy Crystal got into the act when he jokingly confused *The Firm* with another best-seller, *Jurassic Park*: "Yes, I read the book and the dinosaurs were terrific" (DeTurenne 206)!

A few reviewers, seemingly all New York-based, didn't like the novel at all. Marilyn Stasio of the *New York Times* called Mitch McDeere "a money-grubbing worm," adding that "if [that's] what passes for a hero in today's legal profession, we'll stick with Portia" (7). The *New Yorker* was even more caustic in its comments. Answering the question "Why do . . . [people] read John Grisham?" the reviewer observed, "They say that he forces you to keep on flipping the pages, but then so does a Rolodex." The reviewer objected most strenuously to the novel's plot, and later to the plot of the film based on the novel. He writes that when he realized that the pivotal event of *The Firm* was going to involve photocopying, he thought, "Oh, well . . . the screen version will change all that, beef things up a little, trade the copier for a pair of helicopter gunships. But no—the lure of office machinery proved too strong" (Lane 151). Pagan Kennedy in the *Village Voice*, meanwhile, snidely observed that "*The Firm* is free of the literary oat bran of social commentary; instead it serves up a delicious pate of designer labels, schlocky suspense, and six-figure salaries" (Kennedy S7). Certainly, to appreciate Grisham's novel, readers need to be familiar with images from popular culture. A BMW 318i, Volvos, Peugeots, Saabs, Hartman luggage, former New York Jet quarterback Joe Namath, James Earl Ray, Colonel Sanders, Canon copiers, recording artist Bruce Springsteen, Duckhead clothing, Juicy Fruit chewing gum, Roi-Tan cigars, Gold Mastercard, the Bombay Bicycle Club bar and restaurant, and Diet Coke figure prominently in the action.

Along with reviewers of *The Firm*, readers in droves have bought, read, and discussed the novel. Millions have also paid to see Sidney Pollack's film version of the story.

CHARACTER DEVELOPMENT

Characters in *The Firm* are not fully developed; that is, readers know them more as types than as real human beings. Mitch McDeere comes from a poor family and has worked hard to achieve success as a football player, student, and lawyer. We know he needs money and that he is persuaded to join Bendini, Lambert & Locke by promises of a high salary and numerous benefits. We don't, however, know much about the inner workings of Mitch's mind: what he thinks and dreams about. We also don't know how he thinks or what he values other than the trappings of professional success.

Although Mitch is undeveloped, he shares several obvious qualities with Jake Brigance in Grisham's first novel, *A Time to Kill*. Both Mitch and Jake come from modest homes. Although Mitch and his two brothers grew up in poverty, Jake spent his childhood in a no-frills rural southern home. Both were football quarterbacks. Both went to law school. Both practice law in the South.

Readers are given even less information about Mitch's wife, Abby, although she resembles Jake's wife, Carla, in that she is tolerant of her husband's work obsession, is agreeable to enthusiastic about having sex with her husband, and has close ties to her parents despite Mitch's discomfort with them.

Typical of most southern male writers, Grisham puts Abby on a pedestal where she is more likely to be imprisoned than venerated. Like Mitch, she is a flat rather than round character. Abby may wonder about things, but she listens carefully and with good will to what she's told. For example, in a conversation with Kay Quin, the wife of an associate of Mitch's from the firm, Kay tells Abby what the organization allows and forbids. Abby responds by repeating the word "forbidden" to herself, but not until later does she question the idea of a company governing the behavior of employees' spouses (26).

Evil is represented by members of Bendini, Lambert & Locke and by the crime family that controls the firm. Oliver Lambert, the firm's senior partner, embodies the firm's corrupt values, bigotry, and misogyny. Royce McKnight, managing partner at the firm, bears responsibility for the firm's day-to-day dishonest dealings. The partner responsible for Mitch's indoctrination into the firm, Avery Tolar, is depicted as weak and vulnerable to both alcohol and sex. Even Lamar Quin, Mitch's closest friend at Bendini, Lambert & Locke, is associated with evil although he is not yet a partner. When two associates in the organization, Marty Kozinski and Joe Hodge, die mysteriously in the Caribbean, Grisham implies that Lamar is aware the firm is implicated in their deaths. Perhaps the most evil member of the operation is DeVasher, head of security. The image of amorality, DeVasher calmly gathers information about the firm's employees, blackmails Mitch, and carries out the wishes of the firm's partners. Although the Morolto crime family barely appears in the novel, they are behind the firm's illegal operations.

Although the FBI should be on the side of good, it appears more incompetent than anything else. The agency promises Mitch secrecy and security, but a leak in its office puts Mitch and Abby in danger.

PLOT DEVELOPMENT

Freed from concerns about characterization, Grisham focuses on plotting his novel, creating its "pattern of events," its "intellectual formulation about the relations among ... incidents" rather than telling the story chronologically (Holman and Harmon 361). *The Firm* uses a standard dramatic structure to create suspense. That structure has five phases: introduction, rising action, climax or crisis, falling action, and catastrophe (Holman and Harmon 153).

In the novel's introduction, which "creates the tone, gives the setting, introduces the characters, and supplies other facts necessary to understand" (Holman and Harmon 153), Grisham sets the scene, bringing Mitch and Abby into it. Readers learn first of Mitch's Boston interview with firm members, and we hear Mitch discuss the interview with Abby. Grisham next lets us visit Memphis with Mitch and Abby as they look over the firm's offices and the town in which they will live.

The rising action (in this case the emergence of evil as embodied in Bendini, Lambert & Locke) begins in Chapter 3 as readers—and, later, Mitch—begin to suspect that the firm engages in shady business practices. Grisham first describes the fifth floor of the Bendini building where the security offices are located; he indicates that DeVasher, head of security, gathers seemingly irrelevant information about the McDeeres, having wiretapped their hotel room. Before long, readers learn that two members of the firm have just died in a suspicious diving accident in the Grand Caymans, and Mitch senses that firm member Lamar Quin is less than satisfied with his position at Bendini, Lambert & Locke. Nevertheless, Grisham shows Mitch McDeere to be a devoted employee, heading into the office before dawn and staying there until very late. Abby's frustration mounts as she sees her marriage endangered by her husband's obsession with his career. Meanwhile, readers watch as the firm wiretaps the McDeeres' home, and we grow fearful as we learn that at least five other associates in the organization have died under mysterious circumstances. Suspense is running high, therefore, even before Wayne Tarrance of the FBI reveals to Mitch that the firm is under FBI surveillance for possible illegal activities and before Eddie Lomax, the detective whom Mitch hires to look into his situation, is murdered.

The climax of Grisham's novel occurs when Mitch realizes for the first time how much trouble he's in. This realization occurs after Mitch accompanies Avery Tolar to the Grand Caymans, has sexual intercourse with a woman on the beach, then learns the firm has photographed him and threatens to show the pictures to Abby.

The falling action, that which "stresses the activity of the forces opposing the hero" (Holman and Harmon 153) as well as the protagonist's actions to thwart those forces, occurs as Mitch, Mitch's brother Ray, and Abby dart about the southern coast of the United States with firm members, Morolto family, and the FBI in pursuit. Abby and the dead detective's secretary, Tammy Hemphill, also figure prominently in this part of the novel when Mitch carries documents out of the firm for Tammy to copy, and Abby and Tammy journey to the Caymans to copy secret documents being stored at the firm's condominium. At first Mitch seems paralyzed by his predicament, taking a Christmas trip to Florida to see his mother even though Abby has gone home to visit her family. Gradually, however, Mitch seems able to collect himself and negotiate a settlement with the FBI (one that involves freeing Mitch's brother Ray from prison and that carries Mitch, Abby, and Ray to the Florida coast, from which they plan to escape).

Whether or not the ending of *The Firm* constitutes a catastrophe is a subjective call. Depending on one's point of view, a catastrophe—or at least a resolution—occurs after Mitch, Abby, and Ray have made their way to safety on a remote island. Readers learn as well what happens to the firm and its cast of evil litigators.

One of Grisham's methods of creating suspense in *The Firm* is to juxtapose parallel events occurring to different characters within a single chapter. For example, Grisham breaks Chapter 2, only 20 pages, into five unnumbered episodes that, as a package, describe the McDeeres' pre-employment visit to Memphis. Episodes 1, 3, and 5 focus on Mitch's conversations at Bendini, Lambert & Locke. Episodes 2 and 4 show Abby, while touring the city with Kay Quin, learning some of the same things Mitch does. In episode 1, Mitch is told about company benefits, but he also hears information that probably should have sent up red flags. Information about the firm, he's told, is private; nothing leaves the office. "Wives were told not to ask, or were lied to" (18). Abby, too, misses signs of danger, eating brunch with Kay in episode 2 and lunch with her in episode 4. In episode 2, Abby hears from Kay that there are no women associates, that the firm "encourages" wives to bear children but doesn't "meddle" (25–27). Mitch eats lunch with the associates in episode 3, where, if he had been looking, he could have seen that the power and opulence of the firm are based on the oppression and poverty of others (in this instance as represented by the firm's cook, Jessie

Frances, and her server-husband, Roosevelt). In episode 5, Mitch learns more about company benefits, details that ensure his decision to go to work for the firm. Most chapters have three to seven (as few as one and as many as eight) related episodes that heighten tension by juxtaposition.

Another plot device Grisham uses to increase suspense is to hint broadly, then reveal to readers, that Bendini, Lambert & Locke is involved in illegal activities and surveillance—all the while withholding such information from his principal characters. Hints of illegality fly over Mitch's and Abby's heads while readers know nearly from the novel's beginning that the couple is in deep trouble. How long will it take the McDeeres to figure out their home is wired? Will Abby find out about Mitch's infidelity? These are questions readers ponder with concern. As episodes in short chapters alternate between pursuer and pursued and among characters within each group, readers also know more about the people chasing the McDeeres than they know about the McDeeres' plans to elude their assorted enemies. Grisham withholds information about how Mitch, Abby, and Ray will escape from the Sea Gull's Rest Motel in Panama City Beach. Not until Barry Abanks shows up in a motorized rubber raft does the significance of a comment Mitch made chapters back about the need to get in touch with Abanks become clear.

Another way that Grisham heightens suspense is by periodically making readers privy to the firm's surveillance activities. By allowing readers onto the firm's fifth floor where DeVasher directs espionage for the firm, Grisham places them where Mitch has never been. Armed with proof of the firm's illegality, readers increasingly fear for Mitch's and Abby's safety.

Grisham also uses stylistic devices to heighten suspense. For example, he uses dramatic tags—he presents the dialogue in play form—to speed the reading along. He also frequently ends chapters or episodes within chapters on a suspenseful note. When Tammy calls Abby from the Cayman Islands condominium where she is copying documents while a drugged Avery Tolar sleeps close by, Grisham tells us at the end of the scene that a recorder has clicked on to tape the conversation, leaving readers to await nervously the consequences of that small mechanical action.

Like *A Time to Kill*, suspense in *The Firm* is based on Grisham's pitting the forces of good against those of evil. Although Mitch is attracted by the glitter of Bendini, Lambert & Locke, he still represents "good." Fresh out of law school, Mitch is full of idealism and uncompromising ethics. He believes in working hard and would not knowingly become involved in anything illegal (129–30). By revealing details about Mitch's poverty-stricken early life, Grisham shows readers why Mitch accepts, with few questions, the firm's attractive employment offer. He barely questions how it can compete for top employees so much more effectively than other, larger firms can.

In the literary tradition of good versus evil, Mitch innocently and temporarily sells his soul to the devilish firm. Even so, as his name suggests, he is "dear": a bootstrap hero who, by his own strenuous efforts, has pulled himself up and into a position of success. Like a "deer," he is temporarily paralyzed by the bright and wicked headlights of Bendini, Lambert & Locke, and Abby is standing in the road with him. Readers, of course, feel sympathy for innocents corrupted or in danger of corruption; suspense increases as we worry whether Mitch and Abby will be able to get out of the fix Mitch has gotten them into.

Although Mitch represents "good" as compared to the firm, he is less than "good" when compared to his wife, Abby, whose efforts to bring down the firm save Mitch's life. She is "good" in that she remains in contact with her parents despite pressures from Mitch to do otherwise. She is faithful to her husband despite his unfaithfulness to her and his many absences from home. In their early days in Memphis, she waits up for him and cooks for him as she patiently tries to accommodate his eager-new-associate's work schedule.

Nathan Locke, local leader of the firm that bears his name, is Mitch's chief adversary and embodies the "evil" that is Bendini, Lambert & Locke. Grisham uses Nathan Locke's consummate evil to increase the novel's suspense. Readers wonder how Mitch, bright as he is, can ever defeat such malevolence. Mitch doesn't even meet Locke until early in the morning of his first day at the office. During this first encounter, Mitch assesses that Locke, who has sneaked up on him, has "the most evil face he has ever encountered" (72). The eyes are terrifying: cold, black, "knowing eyes" with layers of wrinkles around them (72).

Others in the firm are also evil. Certainly Mitch's closest associate, Lamar Quin, is evil in that he knows what the firm represents but does nothing to dissuade Mitch from working there. Head of security De-Vasher, also evil, delights in coordinating surveillance on all company associates. He relishes showing Mitch photos he's had taken of Mitch having sex with a woman on a Cayman Islands beach. With sadistic delight he sends an empty envelope to Mitch's home, reminding Mitch that the envelope could contain photographs for Abby and that his soul belongs to the firm. Oliver Lambert, the firm's senior partner, okays

DeVasher's work with the understanding that he receive all sexually explicit photographs and videos that DeVasher produces. It was Lambert's "mission" to sign Mitch to the firm (3), and it is his job to keep Mitch under control once he becomes an associate.

THEMATIC ISSUES

A principal theme in *The Firm* concerns materialism. Although Grisham seems not to mind easy money, he disapproves of money gained through illegal activities. Mitch and Abby are lured to Memphis and into the small "hell" of Bendini, Lambert & Locke by the promise of wealth. They want things. Not just a generic home and car, they crave a particular home in a particular neighborhood; a BMW and a Peugeot, not a Buick; Cole-Haan shoes, not Thom McCanns; $1,500 hand-tailored suits, not ready-to-wear clothing items. By the time Mitch and Abby realize that the money they would use to obtain these items is tainted, they are barely able to survive the trouble they are in.

Grisham further distinguishes between money gotten illegally from honest people versus that gotten from thieves. After all, at the end of the novel Mitch is rich, having earned a million dollars from the FBI and having transferred to his account $10 million of the firm's laundered funds. Nevertheless, Mitch has fulfilled his contract with the FBI and has earned the million from them. Because the $10 million from the firm was stolen by thieves from thieves, Grisham evidently feels Mitch's character remains unstained despite the new-found wealth. True to the Robin Hood myth, Mitch even gives away a few million dollars (442).

A second theme—that the world is a dangerous place—confirms readers' suspicions that each of us must be on the lookout for things that will harm or corrupt us. Even Harvard Law School graduates like Mitch McDeere are not exempt from harm, nor are their beautiful spouses. There is probably some consolation in knowing that no one is exempt from such perils, that danger lurks for one and all.

A question that *The Firm* poses is whether cheating is ever justified. Grisham offers a qualified no. While counting his billable hours and deciding whether to be faithful to his wife, Mitch encounters numerous opportunities to cheat. Grisham seems to say in *The Firm* that professional and personal integrity are linked and that there is always a cost attached to dishonesty, a cost that Mitch is at least once willing to pay.

It is worth noting, by the way, that Mitch's character flaw is arrogance more than greed. Although Grisham seems to want readers to conclude that Mitch seeks material comforts because he was deprived of them as a child, that he wants an expensive professional wardrobe because he owned only hand-me-down coats as a little boy, Mitch's motivations are probably more complicated than that. More than material things, Mitch wants confirmation that he is as good as he thinks he is: he wants to test his skills on the edge of the abyss, always aware that a single misstep will mean disaster.

But *The Firm* affords readers a positive message despite its otherwise bleak outlook. It reassures readers that regardless of whether we've made a mistake, by sheer guts and a little interference from our loved ones and friends we can survive. Even though Mitch sins against Abby and is tempted to compromise himself for material gain, his wife and Tammy Hemphill, the secretary of a private detective, help him escape harm.

There are those, however, who may want to argue that Mitch represents less than "qualified good." A columnist in the *Atlanta Constitution* sees the novel as "morally ambiguous" and Mitch as hardly a hero. He points out that in the course of a few days, the hero

> refuses to cooperate with a government investigation of the Mob . . . , he is an accessory to murder, he is guilty of obstruction of justice, he extorts $750,000 from the government (that's our money), he breaks his murderer brother out of jail and, just to round things out, is unfaithful to his wife. (Franklin A15)

Such a world of peculiar morality, the reviewer concludes, is villainous. In it individuals owe nothing to the community, and everything the community does is corrupt.

A FEMINIST READING OF *THE FIRM*

Feminist criticism began during the late 1960s in response to the assumption that the "representative reader, writer, and critic of Western literature is male" (Showalter 3). This critical approach, developed by women involved in literature and academia, was part of the international women's movement. The goal of both literary approach and social movement was to help women make connections between their work and their lives. By looking at the marginalized roles of women in literature, women scholars could see the limited and secondary roles they occupied on campus and at home.

Feminist criticism establishes gender as a criterion for literary analysis. It asserts that women and men read differently. Women have different experiences from men; women "bring different perceptions and expectations to their literary experiences" (Showalter 3). Feminist criticism also asserts that women's stories are just as important as men's. This critical approach applies to all literature, not just those works written by women and included in our "literary heritage."

Feminist criticism does not come from a "single system of thought," as most other critical approaches do. Unlike linguistic, Freudian, or Marxist criticism, feminist criticism doesn't depend on just one "authority figure or a body of sacred texts" (Showalter 4). Instead, it is an evolving critical approach that encompasses other disciplines such as history, sociology, psychology, and anthropology. Feminist critics don't always do purely "feminist" criticism; instead, they do Marxist feminist criticism, or feminist psychoanalytic criticism, or feminist philosophical studies.

Just as feminist criticism has evolved from several sources, it has evolved through several stages. Showalter names three, the first of which concerns our analysis of *The Firm*. In this first stage, says Showalter, feminist criticism, or feminist critique as she calls it, focused on the misogyny (hatred of women) of literary practices that included stereotyping women as "angels or monsters," excluding "women from literary history," and exposing "the literary abuse or textual harassment of women in classic and popular male literature" (5). The importance of this scrutiny was that it showed parallels between the mistreatment of women in literature and that of women in society. Such mistreatments include pornography, rape, and domestic violence. Heightened sensitivity to the mistreatment of women, according to Showalter, makes sexism and misogyny in both literature and society inexcusable.

Both feminist readings of *The Firm* presented below grow out of stage-one criticism. The first reading points to female stereotyping in the novel. The second locates in *The Firm* one potentially positive and one negative theme pertaining to women.

Certainly, a cursory reading of the novel shows women in a negative light. Bendini, Lambert & Locke has no women associates and only carefully selected female secretaries. Although these secretaries are noted for their competence, they are, according to Lamar Quin, Mitch's closest colleague in the firm, "a bunch of cows" (22): plump not pretty. In the world of the firm, women can't be both. The firm never hires a secretary under age 30, so the associates won't be tempted to philander, the assumption being that women over age 30 are incapable of attracting male glances.

Wives in *The Firm* are, first and foremost, homemakers. Although they aren't "forbidden" to work outside the home, they are encouraged to do traditional kinds of female volunteer work and community service rather than to seek paid employment. Lamar's wife, Kay, is active in the Memphis garden club, volunteers for the heart fund, and is active in PTA and church work (25–26). Women are encouraged by the firm to have children to tie them further to traditional homemaking roles. Because profits are the firm's ultimate goal, its partners want their associates to be happy—and they believe that a happy lawyer comes from a happy home. Wives, then, indirectly serve at the behest and instruction of Bendini, Lambert & Locke. According to Kay Quin, the firm once tried to add a female attorney to its ranks, but she was a "real bitch" who eventually was mysteriously killed in a hit-and-run automobile accident (32). That she should die horribly may seem fitting, since she "thought every man alive was a sexist and it was her mission in life to eliminate discrimination" (108). Two partners allegedly retired early because of her, and one had a heart attack.

Although Mitch never fully fits into Bendini, Lambert & Locke, his views of marriage rather closely parallel the firm's. Despite Abby's plucky attitude—she eventually tells Mitch she'd be "damned" if a bunch of lawyers were going to make decisions about her personal life (41)—she is fairly passive in the marriage. It's plain that Mitch prefers things this way. Mitch values Abby for her long, lean legs, long hair, and middle-class roots, not for sharing in an equal partnership with him. While Mitch works 80–hour weeks, Abby patiently cooks candlelight dinners for him and waits for him to come home. Abby bows to Mitch when it comes to deciding how close a relationship to maintain with her parents. For example, she asks him tentatively if they could stop at her parents' home in Kentucky when they move from Boston to Memphis, but Mitch makes a point of taking a southern route so they won't come close to where Abby's parents live. Abby doesn't press him. When her parents come to visit them in their new home, Abby has to promise Mitch they won't stay long. She often calls her mother collect so Mitch won't know she's been in touch (138). As tension mounts for Mitch at work, he speaks rudely to Abby, telling her "somewhat shortly" to do this or that (81). In the Grand Caymans, Mitch is "tricked" into having sex with a young woman on a beach, an act he never confesses to Abby. Of course, there are lots of things that associates in the firm never tell their wives.

Other, less important women in the novel are depicted as unattractive or mean-spirited. Jessie Frances, the firm's black female cook, is described as "huge" and "temperamental" (28). Mitch's personal secretary, Nina Huff, is "temperamental" and "not much to look at" (58). According to Mitch, "it was not difficult to understand why [at age 45] she was still single" (65). Eddie Lomax's secretary, Tammy Hemphill, who eventually saves Mitch's and Abby's lives, is also depicted as verging on physically disgusting. She chews gum incessantly, has "sticky lips" (139), and laps drinks out of cups (140). The female fans who flock to see Tammy's husband impersonate Elvis are described as "lardasses" by Eddie Lomax, the private detective whom Mitch hires to help him figure out what's going on at Bendini, Lambert & Locke (144). Women are occasionally described in the novel as "string bikinis" (154). Women don't "fall for" someone; they are "in heat" over him (154). They "drool" over men who, like Mitch, tell them to "get lost" (155–156). Even Abby and her friend Kay are described as vapid. Getting together for lunch, "they admired each other's outfits and commented on how slim and in general how beautiful and young they were" (183).

The second feminist reading of *The Firm* focuses on why Grisham might have created so many ugly portraits of women and poses the possibility that Grisham wanted to portray Bendini, Lambert & Locke as a world where women are powerless and where values traditionally assigned to men—materialism, rationality, competitiveness, objectivity, and sexual acquisition—are rampant. In other words, *The Firm* might be a feminist morality tale in which readers see the evil that happens in a world where female values are neglected or are out of balance.

One reason to conclude that Grisham intentionally penned such a morality tale is that he has Abby and Tammy Hemphill play such a large role in saving Mitch's life. They (especially Tammy) put themselves in danger, laboring diligently all night copying firm files in the Caymans while Avery Tolar, whom they've drugged, sleeps nearby. In effect, Grisham reverses the usual female adventure story in which, at the last moment, a male hero rescues the faltering female protagonist.

In *The Firm*, Mitch is the faltering one who must have help. Although all the characters representing "good" in the novel are endangered at some point, the women are as at risk as the men. In helping Mitch collect evidence against the firm, they perform not just competently but downright valiantly. Although Mitch once prissily observes that Tammy "was not much for housework" when he gets to the messy apartment in Nashville they've used for headquarters, Mitch—not Tammy—looks bad (432). She has already cataloged for him her acts of heroism when she tells him she's worked as janitor, secretary, lawyer, banker, whore, and private investigator in helping him out of the trouble he has gotten himself into (406).

If Grisham hoped to show that Bendini, Lambert & Locke allowed male values to dominate at the expense of female ones, if he hoped to restore balance by having Abby and Tammy rescue Mitch, the novel's ending is particularly sad. Far from ending with what one reviewer called "a Caribbean retirement most of us could only dream about," the novel closes all doors to happiness for Abby. At novel's end, she is stuck in the Grand Caymans in an all-male commune comprised of an Australian bank robber, her murdering brother-in-law Ray, and Mitch, who has committed an act of modern-day Robin Hoodism in which he stole from the wealthy Bendini, Lambert & Locke firm and gave to the poor: his mother, his in-laws, Tammy Hemphill, Ray, Abby, and himself (Larson "Bumpy Flight" E6). Far from restoring balance to the all-male law firm in Memphis, they have brought down that firm and then created another kind of masculine bastion in the Cayman Islands. This is not an environment in which the sociable, family-centered Abby could ever be happy. Upon her arrival in the Caymans, Abby sleeps alone and writes letters she'll never mail to her mother and to women friends. Her brother-in-law, Ray, on the other hand, contentedly masters the language of sailing in the same way he learned foreign languages while locked up in prison.

The ultimate outsider, Mitch is happier in the Cayman Islands than he ever would have been at Bendini, Lambert & Locke. He is now the sole focus of his wife's attention to the extent he never could have been in Memphis. Without her birth family, a permanent home, and her career, Abby can do nothing but remain with Mitch; she can no longer visit her parents or even get in touch with them. She mourns the loss of her beautiful house in Memphis, realizing she is unlikely ever again to have anything so stable. Her career as an elementary school teacher is over. Although Mitch's decision not to enter the FBI's witness-protection program is understandable considering the FBI's failure to protect him before he enters the program, the decision ensures that Mitch has family around him and that he maintains the power in his marriage to Abby.

In this light, it's obvious why Mitch doesn't tell Abby about his affair on the beach prior to his putting her identity, even her life, at risk. If he had told her what he'd done, she would have left him and been safe. Now, even if he tells her, she has nowhere to go, because friends of the Morolto family would kill her. When at the end of the novel Abby brings rum punch to Mitch, suggesting they get drunk and make a baby, she implies an acquiescence that spells loneliness, not victory, for her.

The Pelican Brief
(1992)

As happened when he wrote *The Firm*, Grisham got the idea for *The Pelican Brief* during law school, this time in a class on constitutional law. Grisham says, "I have always been intrigued by the far-reaching decisions of the Supreme Court that come on a 5–4 vote. We are talking about a bitterly divided court. We are talking about a one-vote difference where the outcome would be just the opposite" (Will F1). *The Pelican Brief* builds from this fascination with decision making. It also comes from Grisham's interest in everyday people who hit the road because evil forces are pursuing them.

His lawyer-hero this time is a woman named Darby Shaw. A law student at Tulane trying to figure out a puzzling political situation, she feeds into her computer "information on cases pending in the 11 appellate courts around the country" (Clay E6). Her premise in putting together the data is that "greed not ideology" could lead, under certain circumstances, to criminal behavior (Turan F10). The results of her investigation suggest to her the names of people who might want certain members of the Supreme Court eliminated and why that might be so. She puts her speculations into a legal brief, or report, which she nicknames "Pelican" in honor of the endangered bird, and gives it to her constitutional law professor/lover, Thomas Callahan. He carries the document into Washington and hands it to a friend of his who works for the FBI.

What Darby proposes in her 13-page "Pelican" brief is that an eccentric oilman has been driven to committing murder in hopes of controlling the oil beneath some of Louisiana's endangered marshlands. In fact, in the opening chapters of *The Pelican Brief* two justices—Abe Rosenberg, who "bring[s] to mind the late William O. Douglas," and Glenn Jensen, "whose ideology and real-life model, if any, are less easy to pigeon-hole"—are murdered by a mysterious international assassin whose identity is immediately revealed to readers (Drabelle D6). Khamel, as Grisham wryly names the grizzly assassin, shoots Justice Rosenberg, his aide, and his nurse three times each in the head at close range. Then he garrottes Jensen in the balcony of a gay pornographic movie theater. Before anyone realizes, a cover-up that stretches all the way to the White House is under way. Obviously, someone important seeks to protect the wealthy entrepreneur who has engineered the crimes. Not long after handing the "Pelican" brief to an FBI friend, Darby's lover is blown to pieces in a car-bomb explosion intended for her. Darby goes on the run, hiding in the French Quarter of New Orleans, in New York City, and in Washington, D.C. In desperation she realizes she must ally herself with someone in hopes of making public the conspiracy that threatens her life. After several days on the lam she decides to confide in Gray Grantham, a *Washington Post* reporter whom she is nevertheless uncertain whether to trust. Together, despite Darby's early doubts about Grantham's trustworthiness, the two struggle to elude the evil ones who want Darby out of the way and to build a case against the person who arranged the murders.

According to Grisham, he wrote *The Pelican Brief* in three months and then sold it quickly to Warner Brothers. One part of the deal he made with producer-director Alan Pakula was that the amount paid for film rights would be kept secret, although Grisham acknowledges he was paid "a whole lot more" for *The Pelican Brief* than for *The Firm* (Bennett C5). The amount Grisham received was later said to be $1,275,000.

Although Grisham admits he despises doing research, he did some for *The Pelican Brief*. So that his descriptions of action in New Orleans and Washington would be accurate, he pinned street maps of both cities on his wall.

> Last spring he stayed at [Washington D.C.'s] . . . Tabard Inn (he'd read about it in a travel guide), strolled through Dupont Circle, went to the Georgetown University law library, walked along a street in Georgetown where one of the justices in *The*

Pelican Brief lives and dies, and spent an afternoon at the
Washington Post. (Even so, he put windows in the windowless
editorial conference room. "I knew that was wrong," he con-
fessed, "but I had to have the windows for the plot.") Grisham tried to find out the floor plan for the Supreme Court
and the FBI by phone from Mississippi, "but I was pretty
much treated like a terrorist." (Conroy C6)

Mixed reviews of the novel noted several similarities between it and
The Firm. In fact, one reviewer commented that "Grisham's new novel
is as close to its predecessor as you can get without running *The Firm*
through the office copier" (Skow 70). Most reviewers, however, commented on the novel's improbability. Although the *Chicago Tribune* reviewer acknowledged "Grisham knows how to drop hints and red
herrings with the best of them, and he writes good dialogue," he also
said *The Pelican Brief* is "about as believable as an episode of *Mr. Ed*"
(Toobin 14:4). A *Newsweek* reviewer also thought the novel's premise was
improbable: "Why would anyone, even the richest scoundrel in Louisiana, want to kill two justices of the Supreme Court four years before his
case might, *might*, be heard? Why, indeed, when one is 91 and barely
alive and the other is described as erratic [in court votes] at best?" (Press
73). A *Boston Globe* reviewer observed that "Grisham can plot pretty well
and there is truth in details" but objected to Grisham's withholding from
the reader for so long the contents of the "Pelican" brief and therefore
the identity of the murdering oil magnate (Dyer, "Grisham's Pelican"
56). A two-sentence review in *Forbes* equivocates that the novel is "ultra-
absorbing" but "marred . . . by the writer's intrusive politics—environ-
mentalists, 'public-interest' lawyers and liberal judges are saints;
conservatives, big company executives and corporate lawyers are obtuse,
evil or cynically greedy" ("Not for the Birds" 24). A *Spectator* reviewer
was generally positive but complained that the plot "is not quite as horrifying a tale as *The Firm*" in that "it lacks the intimate menace of the
office [setting at Bendini, Lambert & Locke]" (Hawtree 30).

CHARACTER DEVELOPMENT

As in his earlier novels, Grisham does not develop characters in much
detail in *The Pelican Brief*. Readers are not encouraged to conjecture about
any character's motivations, nor is "a main character [in this third novel]

. . . challenged to change . . . to grow out of what he or she was and challenged to become someone . . . more" (Heise 29). Darby Shaw, Grisham's
protagonist in *The Pelican Brief*, is the case in point. Although she changes
disguises frequently and cuts her hair shorter and shorter, she is the
same perky law student at the end of *The Pelican Brief* that she was in
the beginning. The novel focuses on Darby's actions as she avoids those
who would harm her, but it does not show or comment on how being
on the run affects her nor how it "challenged" her to be anything other
than what she was originally.

In fact, Darby Shaw has much in common with *The Firm*'s protagonist,
Mitch McDeere. She is bright and articulate. Even more idealistic than
Mitch (whose idealism centers on a bootstrap philosophy that reassures
him he will succeed if he works hard), Darby's idealism is less self-
absorbed. After graduation she plans to "make a nice living suing chemical companies for trashing the environment" (17). Whereas Mitch ranked
third in his class at Harvard, Darby ranks second in hers at Tulane and is
within spitting distance of first. She holds an undergraduate degree
magna cum laude in biology. Like Mitch, Jake Brigance, and Rudy Baylor,
Darby is not particularly close to her family. Her father died in an air-
plane accident and her mother has remarried and moved away from the
family home in Denver. Darby does not get in touch with her very often.

One principal difference between Darby and Mitch is that Mitch is
married to the consummately supportive Abby, whereas Darby is single.
Still, at the beginning of the novel at least, Darby is not alone. She has
achieved academic honors while engaged in a time-consuming affair
with one of her professors, the alcoholic Thomas Callahan. Besides ac-
companying Callahan to countless bars in the French Quarter, Darby
often must escort Callahan home safely and into bed. The next morning,
she has to wrench her way free of his "boozy reach" so that she's on
time for her law classes (Press 73).

Another difference is that in *The Pelican Brief*, Grisham treats Darby
differently from the way he treats Mitch in *The Firm* or Jake in *A Time
to Kill*. Here is how Darby is introduced:

> For two brutal years now, one of the few pleasures of law
> school had been to watch as she graced the halls and rooms
> with her long legs and baggy sweaters. There was a fabulous
> body in there somewhere they could just tell. But she was not
> one to flaunt it. She was just one of the gang, and adhered to
> the law school dress code of jeans and flannel shirts and old

sweaters and oversized khakis. What they wouldn't give for
a black leather miniskirt. (14)

Although one could explain away the passage's suggestive descriptions
by arguing that these are not Grisham's views but those of the "guys"
sitting in the fourth and fifth rows of Darby's constitutional law class,
every male in the novel views Darby through the same sexual lens. They
note her long legs and red toenail polish—details that distinguish her
from Grisham's male heroes, who receive more decorous treatment.
Mitch, we're told briskly, had "the brains, the ambition, the good looks"
(*The Firm* 1).

Sometimes Darby's dialogue and behavior strain credibility. A *Chicago
Tribune* review quotes Grisham's protagonist "sighing" to FBI agent
Gavin Verheek, "What would you do if you knew you were supposed
to be dead, and the people trying to kill you had assassinated two Supreme Court justices, and knocked off a simple law professor, and they
have billions of dollars which they obviously don't mind killing with?"
(Colbert 14). Such a sentence, one obviously intended to summarize
Darby's situation and reinforce plot, would be difficult to utter in a single
"sigh." One reviewer finds it strange that Darby "change[s] her hair
color and sip[s] fancy coffee at a variety of picturesque New Orleans
locales—something that makes sense only if you view this novel as a
screenplay-in-waiting" (Toobin 14:4). Certainly, Mitch never deigned to
change his hair color; he donned sunglasses and a hat.

Unlike his male lawyer heroes Mitch McDeere and Adam Hall, Grisham gives Darby a best friend, Alice Stark. However, the character seems
contrived. While Darby is on the run, Alice checks on Darby's apartment,
meets Darby at an oyster bar on St. Peter in the French Quarter to convey
her findings, and then drops conveniently out of the plot. The relationship between Darby and Alice seems as improbable as Alice's brief appearance in Grisham's plot. Readers are told Alice has been to Darby's
apartment at least a dozen times, yet she doesn't know there's a hallway
linking it to the apartment nextdoor. When Alice asks where Darby is
staying and Darby answers that she's not staying anywhere in particular
and that she's having to move around a lot, Alice gets up, kisses Darby
on the cheek, and leaves. She offers no suggestions; she expresses no
feelings of fear for her friend. It's as if her role in the plot is complete.

Far from being a female hero for our times as she has been touted,
Darby Shaw is depicted in old-fashioned terms. One reviewer points out
that Darby comes from "the finest tradition of 19th-century fiction" in

that she "is saved from a life of litigation when she drops out of law school perilously close to the bar exam. Honor almost stained is sure fire, and in successive Grisham melodramas, we may expect heroines rescued at the last moment from careers as Congresswomen, TV weather babblers and Tobacco Institute scientists" (Skow 70). However, it's only fair to Grisham to point out that two of his male characters are also saved from "honor stained" by a life at the bar. Mitch McDeere and Rudy Baylor leave behind their law careers at the end of *The Firm* and *The Rainmaker*. So far, at least, Darby is Grisham's only female hero, except for Reggie Love in *The Client*; unlike most of Grisham's lawyer heroes of either sex, Reggie is still practicing law at the end of *The Client*.

As might be expected, other characters in *The Pelican Brief* are even more two-dimensional than Darby. Readers learn little about "good" characters such as Gray Grantham, who is "a serious ethical reporter with just a touch of sleaze" (150). There seems to be little to know about Thomas Callahan, Darby's lover and law professor, other than that he is "a sweetheart, a soft grader, and it was a rare dumbass who flunked" his constitutional law class (15). "Evil" characters are equally sketchily depicted. The president of the United States, a man who would rather play golf than govern, is more concerned about reelection than truth. Fletcher Coal, his balding chief of staff, is a "guileful manipulator" and a "nasty henchman" (36). Evil incarnate in the novel, Victor Mattiece, the Louisiana land baron, resembles Howard Hughes. He is "gaunt," wears only white gym shorts, "has long gray hair and a dirty beard," and is apparently phobic about germs (348).

PLOT DEVELOPMENT

Is the plot of *The Pelican Brief* realistic or not? That is a question several reviewers of the novel address. Some claim the novel's plot is shaky; others enjoy its intrigue. One reviewer, tongue in cheek, reminds readers that any thriller "requires a suspension of disbelief. After all, who could believe a plot in which the CIA and FBI obstruct justice, a White House aide secretly tapes sessions in the oval office, and a big law firm represents sleazy clients simply for the money?" (O'Briant, "Grisham's New Thriller" N8). Regardless, it is true that the plot's believability depends on a fairly shaky premise: that a law student single-handedly can unravel a conspiracy that the above-mentioned agencies and a Republican presidential administration cannot.

Whether or not the main plot is realistic, some peripheral elements of Grisham's story seem implausible. The elderly White House janitor with access to state secrets is an example of this implausibility. An old man pushing a dust mop close enough to overhear top-level meetings stretches the reader's imagination. That such activities could go on for 30 years (that is, through at least four administrations), as Grisham says they have, without arousing suspicion or being detected, seems hardly possible. That the robotic assassin, Khamel, turns to mush at the sight of Darby's photograph and gets killed while holding hands with Darby in line to board the *Bayou Queen* riverboat also surely strains many readers' willingness to believe.

Small plotting mistakes are a reminder of how quickly Grisham wrote this third novel. At one point Fletcher Coal is visiting with L. Matthew Barr, leader of something called the Unit, a group handling the administration's dirty tricks. Coal tells Barr that he suspects a half-blind janitor of sabotage, and he wants Barr to murder him if the suspicion proves true. Barr's response is, "This is great, Coal. We're spending all this money to track blind Negroes" (170). The problem here is that Coal hasn't told Barr that Sarge, the janitor, is black. Unless all White House janitors are black, how could Barr know about Sarge's ethnic background when he's hearing about the man for the first time?

The novel's ending seems less compelling than that of *The Firm*, in which Mitch's brother Ray breaks an assailant's neck so he, Mitch, and Abby can escape. In *The Firm* good and evil enjoy a final face-off, with the forces of good prevailing. Not so in *The Pelican Brief*, where Grisham commits a story-telling error: he leads readers to expect a major climax with Darby coming face-to-face with her adversaries, but "when pay-off time comes, he doesn't deliver the goods. . . . Instead, they [the bad guys] steal into the night once she seeks safety in the confines of the Washington Post building" (Pugh "Pelican" 6). Before we know it, Darby—like Mitch McDeere in *The Firm*—is ensconced in the Virgin Islands, beginning her new life of blue waters and sandy beaches.

In laying out *The Pelican Brief*, Grisham relied on strategies he used in both *A Time to Kill* and *The Firm*. Chapters tend to be even shorter in *The Pelican Brief* than in his first two novels, on average about 9–10 pages. Within each of the novel's 45 chapters are 1–11 scenes or sections that juxtapose events, characters, actions. Because *The Pelican Brief* was likely written with Hollywood in mind, each chapter contains a series of brief but related snapshots. Both Supreme Court justices are killed in a single chapter after their assassin is introduced. The novel's longest chapter somewhat tediously details the efforts by Darby and Gray Grantham to locate a potential source of information; each section of the chapter describes an interview with a person who might be able to identify that source.

Generally, however, the effect of Grisham's method of plot development is to speed things along. The action quickly moves from character to character or situation to situation. Readers can enjoy the novel anywhere and for any length of time. We can take it up for only a minute or two, if we choose. We can, for example, look at a snapshot (that is, read a scene) while boiling water for a macaroni and cheese dinner, standing in line at the bank, or circling an airport while waiting to land. Also, there is variety in each bite-sized piece. One chapter focuses on the scene in Washington, the next on Darby's efforts to hide in New Orleans or New York, making the book easy to put down but tempting to pick up.

As in *A Time to Kill*, Grisham creates suspense in *The Pelican Brief* by focusing on violence in the novel's early pages: the murders of two Supreme Court justices in Washington, D.C., by a cold and methodical assassin. Grisham introduces law professor Thomas Callahan and student Darby Shaw, both from New Orleans. He then turns to the president of the United States and his chief of staff, Fletcher Coal, who seem more concerned with the effects of the Supreme Court justices' deaths on the president's political career than on rooting out the murderer or murderers. All these quick sketches cause readers to wonder how such disparate characters' lives will intersect.

Gradually, events in Washington, D.C., and New Orleans come together as Darby Shaw puzzles over and then suspects she has solved the Supreme Court murders. Her brief, in which she details her hypotheses, finds its way into high places in Washington. Suspense in the novel skyrockets after the car bomb meant for Darby explodes, blowing her lover to pieces. Darby goes on the run, with readers wondering who among a list of possibilities might be trying to kill her. Darby first skulks in disguise around New Orleans until an FBI agent and an assassin tracking her are killed there. Then she flees to Baton Rouge and New York, in the process contacting Gray Grantham for protection.

Meanwhile, to increase suspense, Grisham introduces a further subplot: another source trying to feed information to Grantham. However, this source (a lawyer working in a corrupt law firm) fears for his life, if any of his colleagues should find out what he is doing. Grantham now has three people, including Darby Shaw, leaking information to him. All of it seems to relate to the situation Darby writes about in her brief.

To help Darby, Grantham flies to New York and finds her hiding in the St. Moritz hotel. They join forces, Darby for protection and access to the press Gray Grantham affords her. Grantham, seeking a Pulitzer, wants Darby's story.

Here, midway through the novel, Grisham uncharacteristically interrupts the action to provide background on the environmental issues that have led to the chain of events being described. He also gives readers information about Victor Mattiece, the Howard Hughes act-alike, who may have been behind the Supreme Court murders as well as the attempt on Darby's life. Grisham also tells about the Green Fund, an environmental group trying to stop Mattiece. That Grisham inserts this section so bluntly may reflect the haste with which he says he put the novel together; it also momentarily weakens the suspense he has worked so hard to build.

After this interruption Grisham returns readers to Darby and Gray in New York City, where Darby spills her story to Gray and his tape recorder, reciting the legal details surrounding Mattiece's activities. The two decide to join forces in Washington, D.C., in order to get to the bottom of things. In Washington the suspense never really builds again, even though Darby must continually elude evil forces and, together, Gray and Darby try to locate the attorney source whom they believe has information linked to Darby's Pelican Brief. Gray's hotel room is broken into; Darby does research for Gray, this time without her computer; and the two finally identify the lawyer feeding Grantham information, but he is murdered before they can locate him. However, with luck cooperating, the lawyer's wife gives them the key to a lock box belonging to her husband. There Darby locates the information that links the attorney's law firm to the nefarious dealings of Mattiece. Together Darby and Gray write the story that Gray eventually publishes in the *Washington Post*.

The case all but resolved, Darby still does not feel out of danger. With the help of Gray Grantham, Darby negotiates an escape from Washington, D.C. Readers next see Darby in Charlotte Amelie on St. Thomas, the Virgin Islands. From there she rents a beach house on St. John "where the mountain met the sea" (434). In the islands she at last has time to mourn her dead professor/lover, Thomas Callahan, and to consider whether she ever wants to see Gray Grantham again.

SOCIAL CONTEXTS

Grisham clearly indicts the petroleum industry for what he sees as its arrogant acquisitiveness. He apparently believes that greed—as depicted by Victor Mattiece and others like him—can lead to the weakening, even downfall, of the United States. But what is true at a national level is equally true on a personal level: greed of any sort weakens and destroys. In this context, Grisham doesn't as clearly indict personal acquisitiveness in the form of alcohol consumption. He glamorizes drinking, suggesting that it invariably leads to sex or glory stories about sexual conquests. Thomas Callahan and Gavin Verheek, both alcoholic, are portrayed as larger than life. Each hedonistically lives in the moment.

Callahan, for example, seems to have it all. A glamorous figure, he teaches in a law school, drives an expensive car, and has slept with numerous young female students. Grisham tends to subordinate Callahan's professional success to his personal success, which centers around alcohol and sex. Once, Callahan gets drunk shortly after showing up at Darby's apartment with a bottle of wine and some pizza. Because Darby's been unavailable for three days, Callahan wants to know where she's been; he also wants to make up for lost time—he hasn't had sex in three days. Though Darby is busy figuring out who killed Callahan's idol, Justice Rosenberg, Callahan appears not to be mourning much. Instead, he badgers Darby to have intercourse with him. Although his behavior might seen rude, or at least insensitive, Darby apparently doesn't object at all. She suggests they become half-drunk instead of completely so and soon has sex with him.

Gavin Verheek, Callahan's law school chum, also drinks far more than he should. Although Grisham doesn't glamorize Verheek the way he does Callahan, he portrays Verheek's personal and professional life as unsatisfying. Verheek has been wed three times—he acknowledges having married this last time for money—yet he manages to work 100 hours a week. Verheek's unhappiness shows when he compares his life to Callahan's. Verheek envies his best friend, who works less than half the hours he does yet earns nearly the same salary. Verheek's only happiness seems to come while drinking and swapping stories about sex with his buddy. On one such occasion Verheek tells Callahan that he loves him more than he loves his wife. The sentiment is lost when Callahan accurately points out that that's not saying much.

Perhaps without intending to, Grisham echoes the Tina Turner song

"What's Love Got to Do with It?" Sex and love seem not to have much
to do with each other for certain male characters in the novel. Tina
Turner's question gets posed early in the novel when Justice Jensen is
murdered in the pornographic movie house. Obviously, Jensen's visits
to such a place suggest that he's out looking for sex, not love. Thomas
Callahan is well known among law students at Tulane for his casual
sexual encounters with women. Nevertheless, to her credit, Darby seems
to be seeking love along with a sexual relationship. She sets standards
that her partner must meet. She asks Callahan to be monogamous, not
to tell anyone about their involvement, and not to drink so much. Callahan eagerly agrees to all three, although he doesn't meet all her conditions. He tells Darby before a trip to Washington that he wants to "get
laid" by her, so he won't be tempted to have sex with women while
traveling (87). He also asks Darby to have sex with him to help him deal
with the symptoms of his alcoholism (88).

THEMATIC ISSUES

Most reviewers of *The Pelican Brief* dismiss the possibility that the novel
has much to say by way of theme or message. As one reviewer put it,
The Pelican Brief isn't "about anything in particular. If it takes as its premise that people in power are brutally cynical and manipulative and will
do just about anything to get a leg up, it never questions that view or
explores it even shallowly. Darby's main desire is to get away from it
all to the Caribbean, which in her vision resembles an airline advertise-
ment" (Lehmann-Haupt C22).

Nevertheless, if *The Pelican Brief* seems long on action and short on
theme, it leads readers toward certain global conclusions. Perhaps the
most important of these is that social evils in our society go beyond a
single corrupt law firm, such as the one Grisham wrote about in *The
Firm*. In *The Pelican Brief* corruption seems everywhere: in industry, in
government, and in the newspaper business.

Although Grisham doesn't develop a particular theme about journalistic ethics, he raises issues in *The Pelican Brief* about a journalist's responsibilities. He implicitly asks which is more important: getting at the
truth or getting the big story. By mentioning that Gray Grantham might
be in line to receive a Pulitzer prize, Grisham implies Grantham wants
to expose Mattiece and the president for personal gain. Grisham also
forces readers to question a journalist's responsibilities to a confidential

source. Grantham lies to his lawyer informant Curtis Morgan, a.k.a., Garcia, promising him he isn't tracing Garcia's phone calls, and then sends a photographer to secretly take the man's picture. Garcia has told Grantham he isn't ready to come forward; Grantham, after photographing him, intends to force Garcia to talk whether he wants to or not. Grantham is probably responsible in part for Garcia's death.

Although Grisham probably didn't intend to deliver such a message, he nonetheless suggests that a smart and beautiful woman is dangerous. That is, she'll probably get you killed. According to *Booklist*, "Those to whom she [Darby] imparts her knowledge start dropping like the proverbial winged sextapeds" (Olson 883). Several male characters in *The Pelican Brief* die after coming into contact with the computer-proficient, long-legged, red-haired Darby. Thomas Callahan gets blown to bits and his precious Porsche is burned. Gavin Verheek's larynx is crushed before his assassin shoots him in the right temple to make the death appear to be a suicide. The brains and blood of Khamel, the assassin, pour into the Mississippi River next to the Riverwalk shopping area in New Orleans. Characters closely associated with Grisham's male heroes are less likely to be killed. Despite extreme danger in *The Firm*, Mitch's wife, Abby, and friend, Tammy, survive an extremely dangerous reconnaissance mission to the Grand Caymans.

Finally, Grisham may be putting forward in *The Pelican Brief* a philosophy of sorts. He seems to be saying that today is the first day of the rest of our lives: we should separate our past and our future from the present and think about how we will enjoy the current moment. At the end of the novel, Darby's life is in danger and it will continue to be. She will never return to law school, nor will she be able to enjoy a legal career as an advocate for the environment. At novel's end, when Darby flies out of Washington even the pilot doesn't know where he's taking her. Cut off from her past, Darby is reluctant to shape a future. For days she lives anonymously in downtown Charlotte Amalie on St. Thomas before renting a beach house. When Gray Grantham joins her, ready to commit to a relationship or even marriage, she tells him they should take things one month at a time.

A MARXIST READING OF *THE PELICAN BRIEF*

Based on the philosophies of Karl Marx, Marxist literary criticism looks at the exploitation of the working class by the capitalist middle class.

Through this exploitation the rich get richer and the poor stay poor. Nevertheless, the poor periodically unite to resist the wealthy. Marx believed that eventually the working class would overthrow capitalism and establish a classless society. Karl Marx, along with Friedrich Engels, expressed these views in the *Communist Manifesto* and in his multi-volumed *Das Kapital*.

Art objects, Marxists believe, are products of "historical forces that can be analyzed by focusing on the material conditions in which they are formed" (Childers and Hentzi 175). As Marxists examine these material conditions, they determine who controls the "capital or means of production by class," including intellectual and cultural properties. A Marxist view of history shows that control of material items is not "passively assumed" by the various classes, and that continual dissension occurs. Just as Marxist critics can study material conditions, they can study the works of art themselves as ideological entities.

> Literature or art signifies the class conflict and Marxist criticism brings this conflict to light as it is articulated in literary texts. Further, Marxist criticism has a political agenda of its own, which is to bring about what it perceives to be progressive political and social change: usually configured as an overthrow of middle-class power (both materially and ideologically) to be replaced with a classless society. (175–176)

Although Marxist critics warn against a kind of "vulgar Marxism" that sees literary texts as " 'reflections' of the specific conflicts of particular eras and their political tendencies" (Childers and Hentzi 176), such activity, though potentially reductive, can shed light on texts in the popular culture such as *The Pelican Brief*. Grisham makes possible a Marxist reading of *The Pelican Brief* by alluding indirectly to *Uncle Tom's Cabin* and its author, Harriet Beecher Stowe. When the director of the FBI, F. Denton Voyles, meets Darby near the end of the novel, his first words are, "So you're the one who started all this" (407). In making this comment Voyles echoes Abraham Lincoln's words to Stowe about her novel, which is credited with arousing public passion against slavery: "So this is the little lady who made this great war."

The Civil War illustrates several of the premises of Marxism. That war culminated more than 40 years of economic, social, and political disagreements between the North and South. It's easy to see how these disagreements occurred. In terms of economics the South was primarily agricultural, producing crops like tobacco, cotton, and sugar cane, whereas the North, mostly industrial, performed financial and commercial services needed for processing the South's cash crops. Although the North and South needed one another, it was difficult for many in the North to understand the South's system of slavery.

Not that everyone in the South practiced slavery. Although the planter class (those who owned slaves) was a comparatively small group, it was central to southern society and politics. Slaves were this group's largest investment, one they needed to protect. Although most Southerners did not own slaves, they were sympathetic to the slaveholders because they feared the slaves would, in Marxist terminology, unite to resist their capitalist oppressors and in the process revolt against them. Because both North and South had capitalist interests to protect, efforts were made to avert a war. The Missouri Compromise of 1820 was drawn up to establish a line separating free and slave states in the land bought through the Louisiana Purchase. The Compromise of 1850 also sought to settle the conflict by allowing new territories to decide whether or not to allow slavery. As U.S. boundaries pushed westward, however, the conflict that Marx would have seen as inevitable got under way again.

Although the Civil War involved exploitation of an enslaved group by a capitalist class, *The Pelican Brief* is about the exploitation of land by that same class. Here big business is presented as a machine that chews up land for profit and injures anyone who won't accept a pay-off or who gets in the way. Victor Mattiece embodies this ruthlessness. Discovering a major oil field in south Louisiana in the late 1970s, he secretly buys up all the land surrounding his "capped wells." Because he wants to "have it all," he "consolidate[s] territory, then dredge[s] yet another channel through the hapless and beleaguered marshlands so that the . . . oil could be brought out in haste" (258). When the oil industry takes a downward turn in the early 1980s, Mattiece devotes his attention to Arab oil until he has cash enough "to gouge his way through the delicate marshes and cypress swamps" of Louisiana (259). All the while, Mattiece "sprinkled money around" to silence politicians who might otherwise oppose his rape of the land.

As during the Civil War, the country is again divided. The division, as portrayed in *The Pelican Brief*, is between industry and the environment as well as between industry and the work force. Curtis Morgan/Garcia, the lawyer who anonymously calls Gray Grantham at the *Washington Post*, represents the exploited working class; White & Blazevich, the firm he works for, represents exploitative industry. Although Morgan doesn't talk much about his work conditions, his widow has plenty to say about them after he's killed. During a phone conversation with Grantham, Mrs. Morgan refers to her late husband's place of employment as a "sweatshop" that works associates to death (368). Any associate still living after seven years, according to Mrs. Morgan, is made a partner in the firm and is privy to all the spoils of exploitation. She's as critical of the partners as she is of the firm. She refers to them as "cutthroats" and "thugs" who intentionally hurt people just to watch them suffer (369). Her husband, on the other hand, she describes as just a good guy who graduated at the top of his class and who worked very hard. The only thing he did wrong was to get recruited by a firm that spends a lot of money putting on an air of respectability but that is actually corrupt and unethical.

Even though White & Blazevich provide a substantial profile of an industry that exploits, the oil company owned by Victor Mattiece provides an even better picture. His company thrives *because of* its exploitations. In that Mattiece engineers all his company's decisions, he also embodies capitalist exploitation. Nothing is beyond his evil reach. He is as willing to kill two Supreme Court justices as he is to desecrate the land near Terrebone Parish, Louisiana. He buys politicians and political favors. Millions of dollars aren't enough for him; he wants billions.

Mattiece's pursuit of oil in Louisiana during the late twentieth century parallels the South's eager production of cash crops during the early nineteenth century. Both industries, as representatives of the capitalist system, willingly compromise others and the land for profit. Mattiece endangers pelicans living in the Louisiana marshlands while he dredges the land for petroleum. The slaveholders in the South exploited Africans to increase production of cotton, tobacco, and sugar cane.

The Green Fund's ideologies in *The Pelican Brief* parallel those of the abolitionists in the North during the Civil War. Both groups object to the forced relocation and inhumane treatment of animals and people. The ends, according to both groups, do not justify the means. The Green Fund is unwilling to let the environment be destroyed so that Mattiece and his company can earn billions, just as the North wasn't willing to support the South's use of slaves to achieve economic success.

Darby Shaw, in *The Pelican Brief*, is the ideal voice for the Green Fund in that she is a lot like the pelican, the endangered bird the law brief is named after. Darby is the voice of the proletariat. She lost her father in a plane crash and has not received adequate compensation for his death. Like others in her family, Darby has been permanently disenfranchised by capitalist machinery. If Mattiece is allowed to continue drilling, the pelican will be hurt or destroyed.

Both Darby Shaw and Harriet Beecher Stowe wrote documents that ask readers to look more closely at economic and moral issues. A Marxist reading of *The Pelican Brief* suggests that a small number of industries, if left unchecked, will compromise the integrity of a government and its people. Profit for the ruling classes, we are reminded, should not be more important than the rights of the rest of us. And that's what Harriet Beecher Stowe said in *Uncle Tom's Cabin* as well.

The Client
(1993)

Just as in *The Pelican Brief*, an ecological issue provides background for John Grisham's fourth novel, *The Client*. This time a U.S. senator who opposes a Mafia-owned toxic dump has been murdered. While police search for his body, Jerome Clifford, attorney for the Louisiana Mafioso who killed the senator, pulls his big, black Lincoln into a wooded clearing in North Memphis, Tennessee, with plans to commit suicide. Here Grisham's hero emerges, an 11-year-old boy named Mark Sway. Mark and his brother Ricky, age 8, have wandered into the woods to smoke cigarettes and are interrupted by the suicidal lawyer's arrival. Already drunk on whiskey, the lawyer runs a hose from the car's exhaust pipe through a window, hoping to die by carbon monoxide poisoning. Realizing the man's intent, Mark crawls on his hands and knees through tall grass and twice pulls the hose out of the exhaust pipe. Twice the drunk attorney, thinking he has botched the job, staggers from his car and puts it back. On Mark's third attempt the man catches him, pulls him into the car, and slaps him around. In fact, Mark nearly dies alongside the person he has tried to save. Inside the car, Mark and Clifford negotiate Mark's fate. Clifford confides in the boy the secret that has ruined his life: he knows where the senator's body is buried. The secret is critical. Without the body, authorities don't have a case against Clifford's Mafia client, Barry "the Blade" Muldanno; with the body they will likely be able to convict and lock away the Blade for a long time. Within minutes Jerome

Clifford shoots himself, leaving Mark Sway, who manages to escape from Clifford's car, as the sole possessor of the secret information.

All these events are laid out in the book's opening pages. The rest of the novel works out the forces that these events have set in motion. Hospitalized with post-traumatic shock syndrome, Mark's brother Ricky lapses into a coma, curled into a fetal position. Mark's mother, 30-year-old Dianne, who is divorced from Mark's alcoholic, abusive father, occupies herself with Ricky's care. Fearful that his brother or mother might be harmed because of what he knows, Mark hires an attorney, 52-year-old Reggie Love, to advise him. Together, the two comprise a cocky and ingenious team. They must elude the New Orleans district attorney and the Mafia, both of whom want to find out how much Mark knows, and they must find a way to keep Mark and his family safe from harm.

Doubleday did a first printing of 1.2 million hardcover copies of *The Client* and the novel quickly topped best-seller lists. Reviewers who praised the novel appreciated Grisham's shift away from espionage and toward juvenile justice, one labeling the novel "a 422–page anxiety attack . . . [that] tap[s] into primal fantasies and primal fears" (Dyer "Back on Track" 56). They enjoyed the novel's plot and some of its characters, particularly Reggie Love and Mark Sway, whom they described as more fully developed than any of Grisham's earlier protagonists. One reviewer commented that "in an age where most novels feature pubescent women or aging male superheroes, it's refreshing to have a heroine who has learned that life only gets better with age and wisdom" (Pugh "Grisham's New Mystery" C4). As for Mark Sway, another reviewer wrote that "all that time [Grisham] spent coaching Little League baseball in Oxford, Mississippi, has really paid off [in that] . . . Grisham's Mark is a convincing, compelling little boy who knows how to make his way in the world. And Grisham knows how to present that wonderful combination of false bravado and real courage that characterizes boys of this age" (Larson "Small Child" E7).

Reviewers who objected to *The Client* did so because they thought the novel's plot implausible and some of its characters unreal. The *Houston Post* described its plot as "wafer-thin" (Pugh "Grisham's New Mystery" C4). The *San Francisco Chronicle* called Barry "the Blade" Muldanno a "flashy thug from Central Casting" (Holt E5). Still, even those who didn't care for the book liked its powerful opening. Even the *New York Times* complimented Grisham for the power with which *The Client*'s early chapters grab readers' attention, claiming they are Grisham's best yet (Maslin C11).

As with Grisham's earlier novels, a brisk auction for movie rights to *The Client* ensued. The rights were sold to New Regency Productions' Arnon Milchan for $2.5 million, double what we know now was paid for Grisham's previous novel, *The Pelican Brief.* Grisham's agent, his negotiator, and his attorney chose Milchan because of the producer's other film projects such as *JFK.* The movie version of *The Client* was eventually directed by Joel Schumacher, who made *Falling Down* and *The Lost Boys.*

CHARACTER DEVELOPMENT

Grisham must take seriously the reviews of his work, because he seems to have worked hard to develop his protagonist heroes in *The Client* (Mark Sway and Reggie Love) more fully than his protagonists in earlier novels. Readers of fiction expect characters who seem real, who do things more or less as they would do under similar circumstances, and who feel the same emotions they would feel. Mark Sway is that kind of character, one whose actions *and* thoughts readers are allowed to share. He is the first of Grisham's protagonists (with the possible exception of Jake Brigance) to have his profile so fully drawn.

Mark seems real because readers are privy to the inner workings of his mind. Grisham depicts Mark as sensitive, reflective, intelligent, and responsible. He thinks about caring for his mother, teaching his brother the things little boys need to know, and being a good son. Though Mark cares for his mother very much—"a bond much deeper than any ordinary mother-son relationship" (52)—he sometimes does things he knows will hurt her. He feels awful when he keeps secrets from her. He regrets teaching his little brother to smoke, although he's proud to have taught Ricky to throw a football and ride a bike. Readers also see Mark ponder moral issues; he spends considerable energy deciding whether to tell the truth and reflecting on the importance of being truthful.

As likable and well crafted as Mark Sway is, some of his behavior strains credibility. Occasionally his back talks seems a bit unrealistic, coming from a little boy whom readers will also see curled up next to Momma Love (Reggie Love's mother) on a porch swing. When, for example, a lawyer's receptionist refuses to get him in for an appointment because his isn't a personal injury case, Mark flippantly responds, "If I get hit by a truck or something, I'll come back to see you" (106). Given a phone for a few minutes in the Memphis detention center, Mark orders

pizza and Chinese food to be sent to the North Precinct police headquarters.

Another reason to distrust Mark's characterization is the television he
watches. Grisham says that Mark watches lots of television and that he
applies the lessons he learns on television to the real-life predicament he
finds himself in. What Mark watches, however—*L. A. Law*, *Perry Mason*
reruns, *Hogan's Heroes*, and *Cheers*—seem more like programs a 30-year-
old man with cable might watch, not a boy living in poverty in a trailer
park. Also, Mark is better able than most adults to apply the lessons of
television to real life. When two FBI agents are interrogating him, he
recognizes from television the good cop–bad cop game they are playing
with him.

Reggie Love is also more interesting than most of Grisham's earlier
protagonists, even if she is less well developed than Mark. Although
readers aren't privy to her thoughts and feelings, we are told a great
deal about her by other characters who have known her for a long time.
"I got tired of writing about bright, young, long-legged protagonists with
perfect teeth," Grisham observed in an effort to explain how Reggie Love
came to be (Donahue "Grisham's Law" D1). Unlike Darby Shaw in *The
Pelican Brief*, about whom readers know little more than how she looks,
how her father died, how much her bank account contains, and what
decisions she makes to elude capture during the novel, readers learn key
events in Reggie Love's past life. Reggie Love is divorced, we're told,
and has lost her children in the settlement. Readers also know Reggie
lives at home with her mother and is a recovering alcohol abuser who
has only in the past five years begun to practice law. She has also filed
for bankruptcy and attempted suicide. Some details help readers make
inferences about Reggie's value system. We're told, for example, that in
her law practice Reggie specializes in helping abused children. Although
none of these details make her complex, they certainly add to her characterization.

Reviewers of *The Client* gave Reggie Love glowing evaluations. Several
noted how pleasurable it was to read about a mature female hero. One
reviewer even suggested that Grisham continue to feature Reggie Love
in subsequent novels, calling her "the best thing about *The Client*" (Pugh
"Grisham's New Mystery" C4). Grisham evidently picked up on the reviewer's suggestion in that he became involved in producing the television series *John Grisham's The Client*.

However, Grisham's efforts to develop his characters end with Mark
and Reggie. The novel's antagonists, the bad guys—in this case some

evil thugs, the grandiose district attorney's office staff, and the bumbling FBI—are one-dimensional. Barry "the Blade" Muldanno's green dress suit has a slimy sheen to it. He wears a gold bracelet and a diamond Rolex watch. The Reverend Roy Foltrigg, U.S. attorney, is a self-absorbed, "oily-voiced, leather-lunged, pious" person who winks at peroxide blondes in restaurants (33). He keeps makeup for interviews in a locked office cabinet. Larry Trumann and Jason McThune from the FBI intentionally violate Mark's rights by interrogating him without his mother or attorney present. When Mark, who's been wired to tape the conversation, asks if he needs a lawyer, Trumann tells him that lawyers get in the way and cost too much money.

For a further discussion of Mark and Reggie, see "A Psychoanalytic Reading of *The Client*" later in this chapter.

PLOT DEVELOPMENT AND SETTING

The structure of *The Client*—the story's events as patterned by the author—closely resembles that of Grisham's earlier novels. As in his first three novels, Grisham uses short chapters containing numerous episodes, each advancing the action in some way. He also starts chapters and scenes in the way he has in the past: by immediately referring to a specific character or a particular place. Like Grisham's earlier novels, *The Client* seems to have been written for easy adaptation to film. However, in *The Client* Grisham seems, if anything, to have deemphasized plot to focus on characterization. His usual technique of juxtaposing events within a chapter doesn't seem as carefully crafted. In Chapter 18, for example, Grisham includes three scenes, but all concern Mark's dinner with Momma Love, Reggie Love's mother. Grisham usually cuts back and forth between characters and events in his plot, using the interruptions to speed his novels' pace and heighten suspense.

Grisham also doesn't use as many scenes per chapter in *The Client* as in his earlier novels, focusing instead for a longer time on a particular set of characters. This slows the action, an effect several reviewers described as "plodding." Reviewers also noted the novel's length, "twice as long as it should be," that they felt "mired[d] down an otherwise engrossing fictional look at the American legal system at work, for better or worse" (Holt E5).

Given the novel's longer length and slower pace, the relationship between Mark and Reggie may be what keeps readers turning pages. By pairing the two characters, Grisham establishes tension between them. Because literature in the traditional canon almost invariably shows male heroes saving females from harm, readers may wonder, given Grisham's older female hero and younger male one, who will rescue whom. There is also something of a battle of wits going on between Reggie and Mark. Both characters have sharp minds and tongues, causing readers to be curious about who will dominate the relationship.

But more than Mark and Reggie's relationship keeps readers turning pages. As he does in *A Time to Kill* and *The Pelican Brief*, Grisham begins *The Client* with a violent scene. This time the violence is not rape or murder, but suicide. Attorney Jerome Clifford shoots himself in the head after threatening to kill the very person who has tried to prevent his death.

Grisham also maintains tension by introducing Barry "the Blade" Muldanno, the New Orleans thug who was Clifford's client and whose actions have led Clifford to kill himself. Muldanno has murdered a U.S. senator and only he, Clifford, and Mark Sway know where the body is buried—information that U.S. Attorney Roy Foltrigg desperately needs if he is to put Muldanno away.

In subsequent chapters Grisham maintains suspense by developing four related plot lines: Ricky Sway's treatment for post-traumatic shock after he witnesses Jerome Clifford's suicide; Mark Sway's developing relationship with his attorney, Reggie Love, and Reggie's efforts to help him; Barry Muldanno's strategies to avoid arrest; and government officials' attempts to question Mark Sway because they believe he knows where the body is buried. Everyone except Ricky Sway is trying to capture or elude someone else. For tension and suspense, Grisham relies on readers' affection for Mark Sway and our desire to see the 11-year-old's safety protected. Of course, Mark is at risk; the government wants him locked up until he confesses what he knows, and Muldanno wants him out of the way or at least silent.

Threats to Mark's safety—a thug who corners him on a hospital elevator, and an explosion that destroys the Sways' trailer—prove that Mark needs protection. Soon he needs protection from the courts as well, especially when he gets locked up in the juvenile detention center for refusing to divulge what he knows.

Perhaps because Grisham can't maintain suspense forever with Mark at home in Memphis, he puts him on the road to New Orleans along with Reggie Love, so the two can find out whether the U.S. senator's body is buried where Jerome Clifford has told Mark it is. This tactic enables Grisham to place Mark and Reggie at the senator's secret burial site. In the darkness, Mark and Reggie search for the senator's shallow grave while assorted dangers swirl about them.

The largest question regarding plot is whether or not events in the novel are plausible, whether or not they could have actually happened. Although The *Boston Globe* claims the book contains "lively social comedy, legal division and at the center . . . an intriguing legal issue" (Dyer "Grisham Back on Track" 49), the *Chicago Tribune* is not so enthusiastic. It catalogs happenings in the novel: Mark is threatened by bad guys; the family trailer is burned; the justice system holds him in contempt for not telling what he knows. How can Mark possibly get out of trouble? "All he has to do is convince his lawyer to help him escape, scare off three Mafia leg-breakers, back down the bungling FBI and work a deal to go into the Witness Protection Program. If all that seems a touch improbable, even for a precocious 11 year old, it is" (Colbert 14:7).

But these aren't the novel's only improbable events. Readers may also wonder why Jerome Clifford, afraid for his life, would commit suicide; why he would confide in an 11-year-old child minutes before doing himself in; why Mark doesn't tell the secret right away to the authorities or to his lawyer; and why the government doesn't immediately volunteer to put Mark and his family in a witness protection program. There are also numerous smaller improbabilities in the novel: Doesn't Dr. Greenway, the hospital physician, have any other cases that prevent him from focusing full-time on Ricky Sway? From hanging around in Ricky's hospital room? Can post-traumatic shock syndrome really put a person into a catatonic trance? As happens in *The Client*, is there a doctor's office anywhere in North America whose staff would actually call a patient's workplace and school, letting officials know that a patient is ill or injured?

Unlike *The Firm*, also set in Memphis, readers barely know they are in a Tennessee river town when they read *The Client*. Most of the novel's action takes place in St. Peter's Hospital, at Momma Love's house, and in assorted law enforcement headquarters in Memphis and New Orleans. After the first chapter set in the woods in North Memphis, Grisham rarely takes his readers outdoors. Even Elvis rates only a reference or two.

THEMATIC ISSUES

The themes in *The Client* are similar to those Grisham has developed in earlier works. Again Grisham pits good against evil, with good (of course) winning out. This time, as in *The Pelican Brief*, evil is organized crime. Although the legal justice system as personified by the Reverend Roy Foltrigg isn't exactly evil, it is incredibly vain. The result is the same; the good characters' faith in the system is sorely tried.

Through Mark Sway's characterization, Grisham may be commenting on goodness in our society. He may be suggesting that the innocence of childhood is purer than that of any adult or social institution, with the possible exception of the wounded Reggie Love. But Grisham may be commenting on more than innocence in his portrayal of Mark. One can conclude from Mark's characterization that Grisham sees more to admire among that much-maligned group, so-called trailer park trash, than he finds among the country's more well-to-do citizens. Mark has more principles than anyone other than Reggie. He does nothing for money, only to help others and to protect his family.

In Reggie Love, Grisham comes close to affirming the value of our nation's legal system. She protects Mark from its most unattractive aspects and for one dollar affords him ample protection. Fortunately there is a judge, Harry Roosevelt, to whom she can appeal in securing justice for her client. Reggie also quietly affirms the values of Alcoholics Anonymous. She lives a day at a time, she works to achieve serenity, and she shows the courage to change what she can.

A PSYCHOANALYTIC READING OF *THE CLIENT*

Psychoanalysis, and thus psychoanalytic criticism, had its beginnings in the late nineteenth century. Its originator, Sigmund Freud, saw in his approach to the study of the human mind (1) a way to study thoughts, feelings, emotions, fantasies, and dreams, (2) a way to gather data about the mind, and (3) a method of treating emotional and psychological problems. Freud's thinking began with a particular illness called hysteria. In hysterical patients a certain symptom would occur—blindness, numbness, paralysis—in an otherwise healthy body. Freud believed the symptoms were generated by an emotional problem: usually a horrifying and forgotten memory, or an uncomfortable unconscious desire. He theorized that if patients understood the memory or desire that generated the symptom, the symptom might eventually go away. The process of exploring early memories and desires leading to a cure for symptoms is called psychoanalysis.

Note, however, that Freud looked at a person's *early* memories and desires. According to psychoanalytic theory, humans are born with instinctual drives that affect us even though we may not be conscious of them. Unchecked, these drives (one toward sexual pleasure, and the other toward aggression) cause us to behave in infantile ways. The drive toward sexual pleasure, or libido as it is called, manifests itself in three stages. The first, the oral stage, involves the mouth and sucking. The second, the anal stage, concerns the anus and the pleasurable sensation of bowel movements. The third stage is the phallic, which occurs when humans first realize that touching the genitalia affords a pleasurable sensation. Youngsters in all three stages tend to associate the three drives with the parent of the opposite sex, leading from the child's point of view to an eroticized relationship with that parent. In boys this has come to be called the Oedipal stage of development, in girls the parallel stage is called the Electra. Parents, in an effort to maintain healthy relationships with their children, encourage them to repress these feelings, to move them from the conscious to the unconscious mind. That is where the terms "id," "ego," and "superego" come into play. The human mind contains all three elements. The id holds all our repressed desires and instincts and is largely unconscious. The superego, wholly conscious, houses the values and ideals society has taught us, whereas the ego mediates between these two. Mostly conscious, the ego directs our behavior, guiding us despite the sometimes contrary voices of the id and superego.

Humans develop through the oral, anal, and phallic stages. A person must navigate through each stage if he or she is going to move successfully toward maturity and mature sexuality. If the transition does not occur smoothly, difficulties—usually anxiety and depression—can result. These conditions manifest themselves as neurotic symptoms and have led people to seek psychotherapy, in which the analyst or therapist tries to uncover the underlying problem. Using what has been labeled "the talking cure," analysts lead patients back in time to revisit those early experiences of pain and suffering. The therapy builds from the hypothesis that if patients confront painful events and share the experience through transference (a form of sharing with the analyst), the patient may be cured or helped to deal more effectively with both present and past. The belief that confronting a painful memory from one's past leads to a healthier present lies at the core of psychoanalytic practice.

Of course, symptoms can sometimes show themselves during sleep when the boundaries among the id, ego, and superego tend to be fluid. Disturbing images from dreams and nightmares may remain in a person's mind, and that person may eventually try to communicate his or her pain using those images. Some of these efforts may result in art.

Psychoanalytic criticism grows out of an interest in how mental processes lead to the creation of art and how that art shapes a particular culture. Freud was interested in the intersection between art, society, and psychology—that is, what happens if many people within a culture share the same dreams and conjure up similar images while daydreaming. Freud believed that "literature reveals certain psychological mechanisms at work . . . and he returned repeatedly to what he perceived as the natural affinity between psychoanalysis and works of art" (Childers and Hentzi 246). More recent psychoanalytic critics look in "literary works not so much for a central 'point,' as for a central fantasy or daydream, familiar from couch or clinic, particular manifestations of which occur all through the text" (Holland 7). Popular culture, just like more traditional forms of literature, is a good site for observing the psychological patterns Freud described. Tracing Freudian images can sometimes lead readers to a deeper understanding of a particular psychological concept as well as a stronger appreciation of a literary work.

Regardless of whether Grisham intentionally created a subtext in *The Client*, a psychoanalytic reading might focus on the infantile world in which Mark reenacts an Oedipal fantasy through his relationship with Reggie Love. Understanding this unconscious motif in *The Client* helps readers appreciate the intense relationship between Mark and Reggie in the closing chapters of the novel. It also gives readers insight into Mark's heroism, which works on at least two levels. On a surface level Mark bravely faces off against the bad guys; on a psychological level he successfully passes from the Oedipal stage into latency, a stage of development that precedes puberty.

Orality provides a backdrop for Mark's psychological journey. According to Holland, "the oral phase . . . [occurs] when self and object are still not clearly differentiated. . . . [T]his first phase is important for establishing our ability to trust external realities, especially other people" (36). In simple terms, each individual must learn to *trust* that the mother, who is the source of nourishment and care, will return even though she disappears periodically from view. Not until we realize the mother is "other" do we recognize that we ourselves are separate human beings. According to Freudian psychology, adults who haven't learned that lesson often "fixate," or get stuck, at the oral stage. Its symptoms include malingering, alcohol and other drug addictions, and fear of as well as desire for engulfment. Engulfment is particularly threatening and attractive to boys who desire yet fend off the consuming attentions of the mother. "The kinds of images in a literary work that would make you expect you are dealing with an oral situation are, naturally enough, almost anything to do with the mouth or with 'taking in': biting, sucking, smoking, inhaling, talking, and the like" (Holland 37). In the female world that Mark occupies in the novel's early pages, all the characters— male and female, bad and good—seem to have had trouble with this stage. Jerome Clifford has had too much to drink when he drives his Lincoln into the woods near Mark and Ricky's home. Drunk, he shoots himself in the mouth. Ricky and Mark also seem orally needy. The reason they are in the woods is to smoke cigarettes. Their mother, we're told, smokes four packs a day. Even Reggie Love bears a wounded psyche. She is a recovering alcoholic for whom the road back to health has been long and painful. It is interesting that Momma Love, Reggie's mother, plies children with great mounds of Italian food as a way of offering love. For Mark to develop into a healthy adult human being, he must successfully navigate this world, learning to love and to trust that certain others won't let him down.

And, indeed, Mark's world *is* female. Mark and his brother haven't reached puberty. Their alcoholic father is absent from the home. Reggie's husband has left too, and her grown son occupies a prison cell, far away, for selling drugs. Although Reggie has a male secretary, Clint, he works in a traditionally female job.

Within that female world the men are dangerous, evil, presenting a phallic threat within an Oedipal triangle where everything is invested in an intimate, trusting relationship with the "mother." The nickname of Grisham's villain is "the Blade," a suitably phallic descriptor. He wears a ponytail and his suits look like the skins of animals. For Mark to navigate the oral world of the mother, he must match wits with this father-figure and win.

Reggie Love becomes Mark's surrogate mother in Grisham's Oedipal drama in large part because Diane is ill-equipped to be a real one. Desperate for legal advice and realizing he can't depend on his mother, Mark trusts his fate to Reggie. Part of the subconscious tension in the novel revolves around whether Reggie Love, her own psyche having been severely wounded, will prove a trustworthy guide for her young client.

The Oedipal nature of Reggie's relationship with Mark becomes especially visible in the final few chapters of the novel. On a psychological level, Mark undergoes a death and rebirth as Reggie's "son." He begins this process in the detention center when, to fool his jailers, he rolls into a fetal position and begins performing the most infantile of all behaviors: sucking his thumb. Fearing that Mark may be suffering the same variety of post-traumatic shock syndrome as his brother, jail staff transport him to the hospital, appropriately named St. Peter's, which can be read as a heavenly send-off and an earthly birth into Reggie's waiting arms. Reggie claims Mark from the hospital, where he has been traversing corridors. More particularly, she conveys him from the morgue, where he's been hiding (a figurative death), across the Mississippi River into life again. Interestingly, Reggie starts referring to Mark as "son" at this point in the novel (466).

But in other ways as well, their relationship becomes more intimate during the Oedipal scenes. Most important, Mark makes the crucial decision to trust Reggie. Hiding in the basement of St. Peter's, Mark telephones Reggie and, before asking for her help, tells her she is the only friend he has. When Mark asks for help, Reggie says the right words: "I'll do anything, Mark," assuring him of her commitment and loyalty to him (452). So complete is Reggie's loyalty that she is willing to risk a felony charge and the loss of her law practice. It's also important that Reggie is with a male, Clint, not Momma Love, when the call from Mark comes in. Though Clint lamely protests, Reggie deserts him for Mark, taking Clint's car and credit cards with her.

The scene with Mark on the floor of the escape car conjures up Oedipal images. The car is, after all, Clint's (the father's) and Mark is "coil[ed] somewhere in the darkness . . . and he remained there until she turned on Union and headed for the river" (457). When Mark suddenly "sprang" onto the seat, readers are given the time, just as new parents are told the time of birth in the delivery room (458). The conversation that follows Mark's "birth" reminds readers of how close the two are. Mark recalls the station her car radio was tuned to the last time he'd been with her. Reggie looks tenderly at Mark and reflects how Mark turns the radio dial with both hands, "just like a kid," and that "he should be home in a warm bed" (459).

To join with the mother in defeating the phallic father is surely the ultimate Oedipal fantasy. Reggie accompanies Mark with a flourish. "Mother" and "son" wear identical Saints caps as they make their first assault on Jerome Clifford's house and the burial site of the slain U.S. senator. Clearly the struggle between Mark and Barry "the Blade" Muldanno, who buried the senator, is man to man, given Muldanno's phallic nickname. The environment they invade is also clearly male Reggie notes as they draw close to Clifford's house where the body is buried, "It was obvious, to her at least, that the house did not have the advantage of a woman living in it" (495). At Clifford's house they discuss wills and death, and Mark reminds Reggie "you're my only friend in the entire world" (497). But this first trip to Clifford's is only a reconnaissance mission. They plan to return after dark to locate the senator's burial site in the garage. Before doing so they nap, inexplicably on one bed, and the narrative comments on their "impossible mission that neither really wanted" (511).

As a successful Oedipal struggle must, their second journey to Clifford's ends with Mark discovering new strength and the mother feeling timid and sadly depleted. The braver Mark gets as he and Reggie forage through the underbrush, the more winded and inept Reggie feels. Repeatedly, Reggie questions why she is doing what she's doing. When she tells Mark that she wants to "get the hell out of here," he patronizes her with the words, "Settle down" (516). More than once he instructs his attorney, now reduced to near idiocy, to "listen" to him (516). He also tells her to "be quiet" (517). Safe in his new strength, Mark even disobeys the "mother's" instructions. Although Reggie tells him to stay with her, Mark crawls off alone in the direction of Jerome Clifford's garage.

Ultimately, in this particular Oedipal struggle, roles get completely reversed; that is, Mark expects Reggie to trust him rather than his trusting her. Mark instructs Reggie to stay still while he locates three rocks he plans to use to alert the neighbors to trouble in Clifford's backyard. Having secured the rocks, Mark crawls back to Reggie feeling confident that "she had not moved a muscle. He knew she could not find her way to the car. He knew she needed him" (518).

Back in the hotel room, however, the original Oedipal relationship is reestablished. Mark takes a quick shower, then curls up on the bed next to Reggie, a proper earth mother with "weeds and grass on the cuffs of her jeans" (532). "She pulled him close to her body, and placed an arm under his wet head. 'I'm all messed up, Reggie' he said softly. 'I don't know what happens next anymore' " (532). Like a good mother, Reggie cradles Mark and he sobs "without shame or embarrassment" (532). Reggie, reasserting her proper role as comforter, observes, "his life was once again in her hands" (533).

The Chamber
(1994)

For a writer who says he hates doing research, Grisham did a lot of it in writing *The Chamber*. This might surprise readers expecting Grisham's usual chase-'em-and-catch-'em tale. In *The Chamber* he offers something different: a thoughtful investigation into capital punishment, a novel that explores from multiple points of view the state's taking of human life. So that he could more realistically recount the weeks before the scheduled execution of the main character, Ku Klux Klan member Sam Cayhall, Grisham visited Parchman penitentiary in Mississippi where many of the events in the novel are set. There he interviewed guards and inmates, spent time in a jail cell, and even sat in a gas chamber. According to Donald Cabana, who was warden of the Mississippi penitentiary from 1984 to 1988 and presided over three executions, the novel portrays events realistically. Cabana adds, "Hopefully it will stir some meaningful debate on the death penalty. . . . I spent my entire career very pro-death penalty, until I had to administer my first . . . [execution]. Now I oppose it" (Mauro 3A).

Doubleday did a first printing of 2.5 million copies of Grisham's fifth novel, the largest fiction first printing in history—and readers responded with gusto. One bookstore chain reported selling 15,000 copies within the first 12 hours, starting at midnight to comply with its Doubleday agreement not to release copies of the book any earlier. In Atlanta, a bookstore named Chapter 11 sold 600 copies during the first 4 hours it was on sale.

That *The Chamber* sold so well may seem surprising, because it is the most unusual of all Grisham's novels. The term "legal thriller," used to describe it, may in fact be a misnomer. Nine months in the writing, the novel concerns the events leading up to the execution of 70-year-old Cayhall, who was convicted 23 years earlier of the murder of two young children. Based on the life of Byron De La Beckwith, murderer of civil rights activist Medgar Evars in the 1960s, the novel is set in Grisham's fictional Ford County, where *A Time to Kill* also takes place. Although *The Chamber* deals with the legal aspects of execution, it is not a legal thriller. Nor was it intended to be. Readers know within the first few pages the identities of the three men who, in 1967, killed the 5-year-old twin sons of Jewish civil rights attorney Marvin Kramer. The boys were playing in their father's Mississippi law office the morning the bomb exploded. Covering the 30 days before Cayhall's scheduled execution on August 8, 1990, the novel details the efforts of the man's attorney to save him. One of the novel's few surprises—and readers know this fact too in the novel's early pages—is the attorney's identity. Adam Hall, the bright 26-year-old pro bono lawyer from Kravitz & Bane in Chicago, is Sam Cayhall's grandson. Even though the tension in the novel is not of the "thrilling" kind, suspense lies in the question of whether Cayhall will receive a stay of execution and the reader's growing curiosity about the relationship between grandfather and grandson.

The Chamber also depicts life on death row. Sam Cayhall and others "eat every meal sitting on their wire bunk, relieve themselves and empty their bowels in toilets and brush their teeth in lavatories, watch TV and listen to radios and the sound of the weeping and railing of other men whose faces they cannot see" (Andig E6:5). Although death may seem preferable to this kind of day-to-day agony, those who defend death row inmates feverishly search for a legal way of saving them.

The novel received mostly positive reviews. The *Boston Globe* called *The Chamber* the *Uncle Tom's Cabin* of capital punishment, an all-out effort to change the way the American people regard the punishment of capital crime (Dyer, "Grisly 'Chamber'" 53). *People* magazine described the novel as a "dark and thoughtful tale pulsing with moral uncertainties" and its characters as "struggling, tormented, [and] too-human" (*People* 26). Lawrence J. Goodrich of the *Christian Science Monitor* also liked the novel: "All the elements that have made Grisham a successful (and rich) writer are here: fine writing, believable characters, social comment, courtroom drama, and legal maneuvers a layman can figure out" (Goodrich "A Race Against a Mississippi Execution" 14). The *Houston Chronicle* applauded Grisham for his change of pace. Although he could have continued turning out "light fare," the reviewer wrote, Grisham chose "an abrupt and perhaps unwelcome" shift in topic and approach (Parks Z22).

But the novel also elicited negative reactions. The *New York Times* found Adam's and Sam's characterizations insincere, even maudlin. Its reviewer resented Adam's untested idealism and prissy behavior. Tongue in cheek, the *New York Times* reviewer commented that when Adam reprimands Sam for using bad language to refer to minorities, "you might want to put the book down and go looking for something high in cholesterol." Although Sam at first seems promisingly unrepentant, the reviewer claims that "he was rooting for the executioner" by the time Sam, "grown mushy under Adam's wholesome rays," started talking about his dog, honey and biscuits, squirrel hunting, and watching the sun rise from his front porch in the good old days (Goodman C27).

At least one review criticized *The Chamber* for being neither thriller nor mainstream novel. Plot threads get left dangling—for example, what happens to the third Klansmember who is presumably stalking Adam?—and suspense in the novel never really builds in the way it does in Grisham's other books. The *Houston Chronicle* reviewer described the novel as "consistently depressing and grim" (Parks Z22), and another reviewer thought it was too long.

CHARACTER DEVELOPMENT

In *Literature: Discovering Ourselves through Great Books*, Joris Heise points out that "a main character is someone challenged to change, challenged to grow out of what he or she was." Heise also says that "such dynamic change marks good literature" (29). If that's the case, then *The Chamber* is Grisham's best book—because not one, but two main characters change markedly by novel's end and because in this novel more than in any of his others, Grisham focuses on character development.

The two protagonists, Sam Cayhall and Adam Hall, are forced to spend 30 days together as Adam uses his novice legal skills in an attempt to save Sam's life. During that time, both characters achieve self-insight. In addition, Adam manages to forgive his grandfather for his crimes against society and family, and Sam learns to care about someone besides himself.

The grandfather's characterization is central to the novel. To ensure success, Grisham had to make readers understand Sam's actions, despise what Sam did, yet somehow see the old man as a salvageable human being. Grisham walks a precarious tightrope toward that goal, and critics disagree as to whether or not he was successful. One who thought Grisham did a good job commented that Sam "could have been a fully repentant old man, now wiser and kinder. He could be mentally or physically ill. Instead he's still rough, crude, and only beginning to feel sorry" (Parks Z22). Others found Sam too transformed. They thought his letters of repentance, as well as his desire to see sunsets and eat Eskimo pies, were evidence that Grisham had slipped into sentimentality; that is, that Grisham had tried too hard to make readers feel sympathetic toward the old curmudgeon.

One aspect of Sam's character that may trouble some readers is his considerable legal ability. Stories of so-called death row lawyers (inmates who have become expert at the law even though they've had little formal schooling) are abundant, but occasionally Sam's contributions to his own defense and to the defense efforts of fellow inmates, as well as his legal posturing in Adam's presence, stretch credibility. One minute Sam asks Adam, "How many nigger partners do you have [at Kravitz & Bane]?" The next he observes, "My, my. Kravitz & Bane, that great bastion of civil justice and liberal political action, does, in fact, discriminate against African-Americans and Female-Americans" (77). Even though Sam's shift in language and tone is intentional, offered by Grisham as evidence of Sam's ironic humor and overall complexity, it is jarring. One wonders whether Sam, obviously adroit with language, would continue to use terms like "nigger" and "kike" as he increased his knowledge of the law and his educational level. Grisham acknowledges that slightly more than half of Parchman's death row inmates are black (32). Wouldn't Sam's community of fellow sufferers have been somewhat less sympathetic than they were about his impending execution had he used ethnic slurs to refer to more than half of them? Why does Sam continue to refer to "niggers" if, among his fellow inmates, there was "generally no real interest in skin color" (111)?

Finally, readers are left with many unanswered questions about Sam's background that might have helped us understand his predicament. Grisham tells us little about his early life, except that he was the fourth generation in his family to belong to the Ku Klux Klan. We're also told he worked in a sawmill and did some farming. Still, readers are left to wonder how Sam developed the anger and hatred that led him to participate in bombings of homes and synagogues. Bigotry does not have a genetic link. Sam's membership in the Ku Klux Klan was not inevitable. His son, Eddie, had a black friend and was anguished by his father's behavior.

Adam's characterization is the critical one, however, because the novel's focus is ultimately on him. Will Adam be able to incorporate new information about his family into his life without letting that information harm him? How big a role does family play in determining our identity? Can we repair the evil that our family has done? What are our obligations to family, and where do those obligations end? For a young man like Adam, who was separated from many of his relatives at an early age and who discovers his family's dirty secret, the need to answer these questions becomes all the more intense.

Perhaps because Grisham concentrates so hard on Adam and Sam, other characters in *The Chamber* receive short shrift—especially Rollie Wedge, the real bomber of the Kramer twins, who lurks around corners throughout the novel yet never jumps out to really scare anyone. Rollie follows people and hatches plots; but like Waldo of Where's Waldo fame, he lurks in the crowd and never does anything. Periodically, Grisham takes him out of storage and places him somewhere in the action.

Adam's adored Aunt Lee also never develops as a character, in part because she disappears during the last quarter of the novel only to reappear at the end, but also because she is never allowed to be anything other than a tool for advancing the plot. She is someone to whom Adam talks and from whom he learns elements of his history. Her unreality as a character crowns when she suddenly shows up close to the end of the novel at her grandmother's tombstone to comfort Adam and, later still, to burn down the old homestead.

Adam's relationship with Lee seems ambiguous, but that ambiguity is never developed. Despite their status as nephew and aunt, and despite their age difference (Adam is 26, Lee is nearly 50), the two sometimes seem to be dating. Adam remembers Lee from his childhood as someone "pretty and cool" who "wore blue jeans and tee shirts" and who walked with him barefoot on the beach in California after his father died. After his father's death they sat together on the end of a pier, where she told him stories about his family and "held his hand and at times patted his knee" (53). In Memphis the two enjoy one another's company over at least one Italian dinner (a sign of considerable sociability in a Grisham novel), and their fancy cars (his Saab and her Jaguar) crisscross town in a potentially meaningful way while he looks for her after she disappears.

They even hold hands when they go back to Clanton, the old home town (251).

As in most of Grisham's earlier novels, the few women characters in *The Chamber* do not fare well. Aunt Lee is alcoholic, but every other woman also seems flawed. Adam's mother has all but deserted him to get on with her life. The female psychiatrist who visits Sam at Parchman is "patronizing" (297). Sam often refers to women as "lard bottoms," whereas the more generous Adam occasionally assesses as "plain" the waitresses who serve him coffee.

PLOT DEVELOPMENT

Whether or not readers of *The Chamber* think the novel is exciting depends on how sympathetic they are to Sam's plight. Suspense here increases if we care whether Sam—an accessory to murder—dies for his deeds. If the reader approves of capital punishment, then the journey through *The Chamber* can be a leisurely trip toward retribution, one that may or may not be interrupted. Readers who are uncertain about capital punishment may feel yanked back and forth by the narrative that makes them first feel sympathy toward Sam and then anger. For the reader who objects to capital punishment, however, the plot serves as a painful reminder of all the complex emotions of people toward both the perpetrators of capital crime and capital punishment.

Although some see the novel's pace as riveting—"Grisham turns his plot into a heart-stopping, down-to-the-wire race, with the clock furiously ticking and the emotional terrain between grandfather and grandson moving like a seesaw" (Coughlin "Chamber" 3), to others *The Chamber* seems to putter along. Certainly, Grisham's premise is compelling: that one family member serves as the sole hope of another who may be guilty of a heinous crime.

Grisham uses the same overall structure in *The Chamber* that he has used in his other novels (chapters divided into separate scenes), but here he uses more chapters, 52, with fewer sections in each. Whereas in earlier works Grisham often jolts the reader quickly between heroes and villains, or between different groups, in *The Chamber* he usually concentrates on a single situation even though he breaks the chapter into several scenes. For example, in Chapter 17 he focuses solely on Adam and his Aunt Lee even though he breaks the episode into two scenes: one where she works, and another at dinner. More often in *The Chamber* than in his other novels, Grisham uses chapters comprised of a single scene. The effect is to slow the novel's movement, giving readers more time to consider the issues.

Another aspect of *The Chamber* that slows its pace is Grisham's extensive use of dialogue. This technique is one way to advance the action of a story, and Grisham uses it to develop background information about Cayhall family history that he needed to work into the plot. Still, whole chapters are devoted to conversations; readers expecting a chase or two and the possibility of a bloody killing will have to revise their expectations or they will be likely to put the novel down.

That does not mean, however, the novel lacks excitement. Grisham begins *The Chamber* with violence just as he does *A Time to Kill*, *The Client*, and *The Pelican Brief*. In the first chapter of *The Chamber* a bomb, placed in the law offices of Mississippi lawyer Marvin Kramer in 1967, explodes and kills his 5-year-old twin sons. Readers know immediately the identity of the killer, Rollie Wedge, and his accomplice, Sam Cayhall. By the third part of Chapter 1, Cayhall has been arrested although Wedge escapes. Chapters 2 and 3 cover a large block of time: from 1967, the aftereffects of the explosion, to 1981, when in a second trial Sam Cayhall is found guilty of two counts of capital murder and "first set foot on death row" (22).

Grisham introduces readers to the second of his two protagonists, Adam Hall, in Chapter 4, maintaining suspense by gradually explaining how this young Chicago lawyer in the 1990s connects to the crime in Mississippi of long ago. Grisham tells us that Adam has gone to work for the law firm of Kravitz & Bane because they once represented Sam Cayhall. Painfully, Adam confides in a colleague in charge of pro bono work, E. Garner Goodman, that Sam Cayhall is his grandfather. Adam tells Goodman he wants to represent his grandfather through the appeals process that precedes any execution.

In the chapters that follow, Grisham alternately focuses on Adam's efforts to obtain a stay of execution for his grandfather and his interest in understanding the relationship between the events that occurred in 1967 and his own identity. In making peace with himself Adam relies principally on his Aunt Lee, with whom he stays in Memphis while commuting south to Parchman penitentiary where his grandfather is imprisoned. Grisham competently creates interest in both stories, allowing their separate threads to interweave through his characterization of Adam.

Adam's gradually developing relationship with his grandfather gives the novel its depth. Although suspense centers around whether Adam will successfully gain a stay of execution for his grandfather, readers also wonder whether Sam will accept Adam's help and whether the two will be able to overcome their differences or even become friends. Thus, we accompany Adam as he talks with the warden, juggles reporters' queries from his temporary office in Memphis, hears the grim stories of others' executions, seeks new information on the murder from an FBI agent, visits the site of the bombings, pleads Sam's case before the governor of Mississippi, and pursues the appeals process step by step, experiencing with Adam considerable uncertainty and dread. We also watch, fascinated, as Adam's anger at and frustration with his grandfather become tempered by a grandson's affection. Adam and Sam spend considerable time together near or on death row, talking about the family and gradually about death.

Although Grisham doesn't as fully succeed in maintaining suspense through his depiction of Adam's relationship with his Aunt Lee, many readers can no doubt identify with Lee's pain, appreciate her kindness to Adam, and worry when she disappears partway through the novel. Adam and Lee also cement a relationship, although theirs develops over Italian dinners, walks in the family cemetery, and a trip to the Cayhall homestead.

As in earlier Grisham novels, a few events in *The Chamber* seem peculiar or improbable. For example, given what Sam says at the end of the novel about repudiating the KKK, why doesn't he now acknowledge publicly that he didn't act alone during the bombings? Why doesn't Sam admit to earlier lynching a boy named Cletus? Throughout the novel he alludes to this other crime, but he doesn't confess it until the novel is in its final pages. Nothing comes of the confession, even though Grisham earlier uses Sam's secret as a way of building suspense.

One of the more enjoyable things Grisham does with plot in *The Chamber* is to refer back to events in *A Time to Kill* and forward to events in *The Rainmaker*. As if *A Time to Kill* were a nonfiction documentary, Grisham has Lee tell Adam about the famous murder trial of Carl Lee Hailey in 1984. Lee reports having "driven down from Memphis one day to watch the spectacle. . . . [Adam] had been a junior at Pepperdine, and had followed it in the papers" (251–252). Grisham's reference to *The Rainmaker* is less obvious. When Adam first tells his colleague at Kravitz & Bane, E. Garner Goodman, that he wants to work on a death penalty case, Goodman responds, "Look, Mr. Hall, this is not the same as counseling winos at a soup kitchen" (27), a service that Grisham's hero in his sixth novel, Rudy Baylor, approximates when he counsels elderly people after lunch at a senior citizens center.

SOCIAL/CULTURAL ISSUES

Grisham claims to be personally struggling with the death penalty issue (Mauro 3A), but in *The Chamber* he appears determined to say two things: (1), capital punishment is wrong because it is wrong to take a life, and (2) Sam Cayhall had no choice but to become a killer. We can tentatively attribute these views to Grisham because Adam, seemingly a version of Grisham, reaches these conclusions. Readers realize that Adam opposes capital punishment when, at the end of the novel, he agrees to leave Kravitz & Bane and work for Hez Kerry's organization, which helped Adam in his efforts to save Sam and his attempts to abolish the death penalty. We sense that Adam sees his grandfather as powerless in the face of stronger forces. Looking at a photograph of a lynching with his grandfather posed beneath the dangling feet of a dead body, Adam sees the clear and beautiful eyes of his grandfather at age 15 and observes: "Sam didn't have a chance. This was the only world he knew" (400).

Despite Grisham's distaste for research, *The Chamber* contains accurate data about capital punishment. For example, Sam knows that in 1989 there were in the United States approximately 2,500 inmates on death row awaiting execution, and that of those only 16 were put to death (168). He also knows that only four people were executed in the state of Mississippi between 1977 and 1989. The one inaccuracy in Grisham's statistics is that no prisoner was executed in Mississippi in 1990, the year the fictional Sam Cayhall awaits his death. Grisham correctly points out why Sam must be executed in a gas chamber instead of by lethal injection, the state's current method of execution. Before July 1, 1984, execution of those convicted of capital crime in Mississippi had to be carried out with lethal gas (U.S. Department of Justice 7:Table 2).

Grisham's horrifyingly detailed descriptions of the execution process are also accurate. What many assume to be a crisp, quick releasing of a cyanide pellet into an execution chamber is something much more hideous. Prisoners are allowed a last conjugal visit. The chamber's lethal qualities are first tested on a white-tailed rabbit. Vaseline must be applied to the chamber windows to prevent gas from leaking into the adjoining witness area. Prisoners' anuses are plugged "so guards won't have to clean up . . . [the dead person's] excrement" (Hartman E8:2). Executed prisoners' poison-soaked clothes are cut from their bodies while they are still strapped to the chair.

THEMATIC ISSUES

The Chamber is a bildungsroman, or apprenticeship novel: one that describes the childhood and young adulthood of a sensitive protagonist who tries to see meaning and pattern in his or her experiences and to figure out how to live well. *The Chamber* traces Adam's development from an inexperienced to a practiced lawyer, from a young man with questions about his family's past to an adult with answers to those questions.

Even as *The Chamber* is a bildungsroman about Adam, it is also a novel about Sam's sin and redemption. Sam's decision to atone for a murder he didn't commit as well as for those he has committed, and his desire to be redeemed for his evil behavior, reflect key themes in both popular and serious literature. Although the *New York Times* delivers its judgment tongue-in-cheek—"*The Chamber* may be read as a tribute to the redemptive value of being sentenced to be gassed"(Goodman C27)—there is wisdom behind the wit. The *Chicago Tribune* affirms this point: "No recent book of fiction has made so strong a statement against capital punishment. And no recent book of fiction has been so unashamedly Christian in its presentation of true penitence and hope for God's mercy" (Cook 14:3). Sam, wanting to get out of his red "monkey suit" before the execution, becomes a Christ figure of sorts, offering salvation for all of us who haven't committed a capital misdeed but who have accumulated a lifetime of petty offenses against God.

Another theme of *The Chamber* is that justice may lurk somewhere in the legal system, but probably not where one would expect to find it. Feelings run high on both sides of the appeals process; and even though Governor McAllister apparently never sincerely entertains the possibility of granting clemency to Sam, the market analysis scheme (carried out by Adam and his supporters in a vain effort to save Sam) probably doesn't reflect justice fairly delivered either. Justice seems to happen in *The Chamber* as a natural working out, as an evolution of the process itself. As happens in *A Time to Kill*, the outcome of *The Chamber* shows that justice ultimately resides in the heart of a single attorney, Adam, who insists on thoroughly representing his client.

Grisham also points out in *The Chamber* that even though Sam is not quite guilty of the crime for which he is about to be executed, he has committed other crimes for which he deserves punishment. Perhaps this is what justice is: a slow but inevitable accounting for the misdeeds of a lifetime.

A further theme of *The Chamber* is that we cannot leave the past behind. As the result of an act of hatred committed by a single individual, an entire family is brought to its knees. A wife learns to hate her husband. A father dies. A sister is forever traumatized. A grandson finds he cannot get on with his life. Throughout *The Chamber* Grisham emphasizes the consequences of our actions, whether we act alone or in a group. "The novel looks at the forces that created Sam, a fourth generation Ku Klux Klan member. And it looks at the violence and destruction that racism does not only to its victims but to its perpetrators" (Donahue "Grisham's Latest" D1).

A NEW HISTORICIST READING OF *THE CHAMBER*

The term "new historicism" was first used in 1982 in a special issue of *Genre*, a journal of literary criticism, to describe "a new kind of historically based [literary] criticism" (Childers and Hentzi 206). New historicism is based primarily on the work of Michel Foucault—architect, historian, and philosopher—but disavows anyone's direct influence (Murfin 155). New historicists believe that people are shaped by social and historical circumstances. In other words, history shapes us; we don't shape it.

New historicists believe that history—the representation of slavery, for example—is not "reliable and unproblematic." In fact, they try to show that history, like literature, is really a version of truth—"a fiction" in other words—and they treat "nonliterary texts"—buildings, artworks, natural objects—as useful in creating that "fiction." Just as history should be taught as if it were as reliable as literature, poems and stories should be taught "in a web of historical conditions" (Murfin 150). The broader context allows us to read and analyze literature, benefiting from recent critical/historical theories such as feminist and psychoanalytic criticism.

Any analysis of history or literature is political and complex. New historicists tend to distrust theories that assume people of a particular age or era experienced no conflicts in thinking. They claim that powerful forces often try to silence those who would disagree, giving the appearance of agreement. Further, thinking of slavery again, "no historical event," we can conclude, "has a single cause; rather, it is intricately connected with a vast web of economic, social, and political factors" (Murfin 153).

According to new historicists, history is not "a body of indisputable, retrievable facts." Instead, history "becomes textualized"; that is, expressed in words or other signs to be read and interpreted by the historian (Childers and Hentzi 207). History is therefore never "objective." Every literary "text"—whether novel, play, or poem—becomes an "account" of the truth, never the truth itself. New historicists are also "less likely to see history as linear and progressive, as something developing toward the present." They remind us "that it is treacherously difficult to reconstruct the past as it really was—rather than as we have been conditioned by our own place and time to believe that it was" (Murfin 152). All historical interpretation is colored by the perspective of the historian. According to Foucault, "it is difficult . . . to see present cultural practices critically from within them, and . . . it is almost impossible to enter bygone ages" (Murfin 153).

Adam in *The Chamber* is a new historicist. Even though Adam's job as an attorney is to save his grandfather's life through legal maneuvering, he spends a considerable portion of the novel trying to make sense of this grandfather's role in a historical event (ethnically motivated murder), historical sites, and a complex period of history, (slavery to the present). All are irrelevant to his grandfather's defense but important to Adam's establishing his own identity. He visits Greenville, the site of the Kramer bombings; spends time in Clanton, where the Cayhalls once lived; and tries in other ways to get a feel for his family and the time more than 20 years ago when his grandfather committed his crimes. Fairly early in the novel, Adam acknowledges to his Aunt Lee that what he is trying to make sense of is "not a simple matter of learning family history" (268).

In his role as historical sleuth, Adam becomes the reader's representative in the novel. Just as Aunt Lee periodically serves as Adam's "tour guide and historian" (251), Adam is ours. Consistent with new historicism, Adam's position in terms of events in the novel is complicated. He is not simply the novel's protagonist. He is not simply an attorney representing a client. Instead, he is enmeshed in the events that happened long before he was born. He is a part of several "networks" described by new historicists that make it impossible for us to understand who we are and how we've become the people we've become. Even so, Adam struggles to arrive at if not truth, then some decision about how to conduct the rest of his life. Adam's decisions to oppose the death penalty and to accept his grandfather's actions as incomprehensible yet inevitable, given Sam's complex history, are steps in that direction.

As Adam struggles to untangle the historical past of a geographical area, not to mention his own personal past, the reader accompanies him. To aid Adam and the reader, Grisham provides an array of data to clarify and complicate the process. Although most of the data are "real" and indisputable, the decisions we make based on them are likely to vary considerably. In presenting his fictional/factual story about capital punishment, Grisham is surely aware that he provides readers in *The Chamber* with one account of the truth and nothing more. We are left to make sense of the data in whatever way we can.

Just as new historicists believe the "text" can be other than a novel, play, or poem, so Adam "reads" numerous texts besides legal documents during his stay in Mississippi. For example, he looks at the houses and headstones of his family. At one point Adam and Lee visit the "Cayhall estate," as Lee ironically labels it. When Adam asks Lee what happened to it, Lee responds, "It was a good house. Didn't have much of a chance though" (252). As Adam tries to "read" the house, Lee lists the other texts she managed to pull from it before the bank foreclosed: "photo albums, keepsakes, yearbooks, Bibles, some of Mother's valuables" (253). At least one such text, a book entitled *Southern Negroes and the Great Depression*, contains photos of the family. Adam eventually uses it to reach peace with his grandfather's situation.

Like new historicists, Adam realizes that he cannot judge his grandfather from a contemporary vantage point and that he cannot make sense of an age gone by. As new historicists would point out, Sam's actions are so enmeshed in the historical and social forces of his time that those of us from yet another time cannot even begin to place blame. In fact, blame is irrelevant. To blame, one must have been bludgeoned by the same social and historical forces, yet have made different choices. Perhaps the climax of Grisham's novel occurs as Adam acknowledges, "How could he fairly judge these people [in the lynching photograph] and their horrible deed when, but for a quirk of fate, he would have been right there in the middle of them had he been born forty years earlier?" (400). Of his grandfather, whose smiling 15-year-old face Adam locates at a lynching in *Southern Negroes and the Great Depression*, Adam acknowledges, "How in God's world could Sam Cayhall have become anything other than himself? He never had a chance" (401).

Why bother to do a new historicist reading of *The Chamber*? Such a reading helps us avoid being aloof from or judgmental about civil rights cases such as Sam Cayhall's. Like Adam, who was originally from California and now lives in Chicago, we too may be caught in the web of ethnic crime. In a larger sense, new historicism reminds us not to place too much faith in objectivity, particularly our own. We are entrapped in a subjectivity we cannot hope to grasp.

The Rainmaker
(1995)

Grisham admits he's never had a real case as exciting as Rudy Baylor's in *The Rainmaker*. Nevertheless, Grisham's first trial was "a heart-stopper": "I was nine months out of law school. . . . The trial was a disaster. . . . I stood up . . . and just apologized for being there. . . . I said my client deserved better than what he got. [I said] 'Please don't hold my performance against him.' And they . . . found him not guilty of murder" (Kelly "Not-So-Trying Times" D1). Grisham's admissions to the jury during this first trial sound a lot like those of his lawyer protagonist in *The Rainmaker*. No wonder the story seems believable, and no wonder Rudy Baylor is so sympathetically portrayed. Grisham has stood in his hero's shoes, and they fit.

In a way, *The Rainmaker* is Grisham's most unusual novel. It is easily his funniest—a refreshing antidote to *The Chamber*, which was somber and thought-provoking. In its comparatively thorough development of character and its first-person narration, *The Rainmaker* is also unlike Grisham's other works that depend on cliff-hanger action. Its protagonist is a likable young man about whom readers learn a considerable amount because he tells his own story.

Rudy, a soon-to-be graduate of the law school at Memphis State University, looks forward to graduation and a job he has been offered at a small local law firm, Broadnax & Speer. When Broadnax & Speer is suddenly bought up by another firm in town, the job offer is withdrawn.

Broke, Rudy must file for bankruptcy and look for a new place to live. To make matters worse his girlfriend, Sara Plankmore, a third-year law student, chooses this moment to break up with him, deciding to marry instead a high school boyfriend, "an Ivy Leaguer, a local blue blood" (24). Sara, we're told, might even be pregnant, a rumor that causes Rudy to vomit when he hears it.

At the time, Rudy is taking a law course called Legal Problems of the Elderly—or Geezer Law by those who aren't able to drop it. It is one of his last miseries before graduation. A course requirement takes him and his classmates to a senior center, Cypress Gardens, to give some pro bono legal advice. During one such session he meets Dot and Buddy Black, whose son, Donny Ray, diagnosed with leukemia, has been denied coverage for a bone marrow transplant by their insurance company, Great Benefit. As a result Donny is near death. Dot shows Rudy a letter from Great Benefit describing her as "stupid, stupid, stupid" for persistently asking the company to cover Donny Ray's claim (18).

With only 38 days until graduation, Rudy at first assumes he'll brush off the Blacks with a letter referring them to a real lawyer. However, an idealistic professor and Rudy's own sense of fairness cause him to reconsider. Rudy agrees to help the Blacks. Because he hasn't yet passed the bar, Rudy arranges for a Memphis law firm to represent his new clients while he does the legwork. When the firm tries to steal the case, Rudy, by now a member of the bar, takes over. He soon finds himself matching legal wits with the insurance company's high-powered litigators. And who represents Great Benefit? Tinley, Britt, Crawford, Mize & St. John, the very company that bought out Broadnax & Speer! Before the case is settled, Rudy faces off in the courtroom against several of that firm's leading litigators—in particular Leo Drummond, whose legal prowess is legendary.

In a series of subplots Rudy maintains a friendship with a law school buddy, Booker, and his wife, Charlene, and helps Birdie Birdsong from the senior center in exchange for free rent of the garage apartment behind her house. Birdie tells Rudy she is very wealthy, and for a while Rudy tries to protect Birdie from her greedy children. To earn money for himself, he bartends at a student hangout called Yogi's and works for a low-life attorney named Bruiser Stone, who has links to the Memphis underworld and whose firm handles both accident and criminal cases. Bruiser assigns Rudy to the hospital beat and hands him a cellular phone: Rudy's job is to sign on injured clients who wish to litigate. Assisting him is another Bruiser Stone employee, Deck Shifflet, who has failed the bar exam six times and refers to himself as a "paralawyer." When Bruiser skips town to avoid federal arrest, Rudy and Deck go into business together. Deck delights in accident work, devotedly pursuing the tragedies of others—everything from automobile accidents to paddle-wheeler disasters on the Mississippi River. Rudy also preys on accident victims, passing time in a local hospital cafeteria on the lookout for injury patients with enough mobility to eat a meal outside their rooms. While lurking over a cafeteria tray, Rudy meets 19-year-old Kelly Riker, hospitalized because her husband beat her. Gradually subplot becomes plot as the hero's relationship with Kelly takes him and readers in a surprising direction.

Along the way, Grisham provides some interesting legal lessons. He describes, for example, how law schools help their graduates find jobs. When the law school placement official contacts a local firm where one of the school's graduates is in charge of recruiting and when the placement official senses that more Ivy Leaguers than locals are being hired, the university president calls on the firm to see that the imbalance is corrected. Grisham also shows how law firms try to win cases by placing minority lawyers on particular cases to bond with a judge sharing the same ethnic background. For example, the law firm of Tinley, Britt assigns its Harvard-educated, African-American associate to the Great Benefit defense team because the judge is also Harvard-educated and African-American. In addition, Grisham defines "fast-tracking," a procedure by which certain cases speed through the system; shows how effective multi-media can be in taking depositions; explains "requests for admissions," a way of forcing the opposition to admit or deny certain facts in a case; and discusses evidentiary depositions and collection law. The novel's plot depends on readers understanding the jury selection process; in particular, they must realize that any contact between lawyer and potential jurors outside the courtroom is a serious ethical violation. Grisham makes all this information clear to his lay audience.

Grisham also instructs readers about insurance, explaining that insurance companies are "exempt from antitrust" and, therefore, have developed accounting methods peculiar to the industry (311). Using this fact as a basic premise, Grisham shows how an insurance company like Great Benefit could scam its clients. He carefully defines for his lay readers Reserve Accounts, Restricted and Unrestricted Surplus, and "dumping," the practice of withholding until the last minute materials requested by the opposition in court cases. He also explains how an insurance company might be able to predict the percentage of clients who would consult an attorney if there were a question about coverage.

More than Grisham's other novels, *The Rainmaker* received shockingly disparate assessments. As with his earlier works, the *New York Times* strongly criticized it. Accusing *The Rainmaker* of lacking "even [Grisham's] patented narrative hooks," the reviewer said the story "gets off to a plodding, colorless start, decelerates into a wholly predictable tale of David and Goliath, and finishes up with a manic flurry of ridiculously implausible events." The reviewer also criticized its lack of characterization and its plot ("a veritable school of red herrings") (Kakutani 33:1).

The *Wall Street Journal* offered a more positive review. According to it, Rudy Baylor is Grisham's "most sympathetic hero" and the novel's plot is his most "engrossing" since *The Firm* (Nolan A12). *USA Today* predicted "*The Rainmaker* will be John Grisham's most popular novel since *The Firm*" (Donahue "Grisham Is Back" 1D).

Regardless of negative critical assessments, *The Rainmaker* immediately made its way to the top of best-seller lists; Doubleday did a first printing of 2.8 million copies, a record number for a first printing of a work of fiction. *The Rainmaker* also seems to be doing well in Hollywood, where Grisham was offered $6 million for movie rights—the same amount he accepted for *A Time to Kill*. *The Rainmaker* sold for $8 million.

POINT OF VIEW

In *The Rainmaker*, Grisham departs for the first time from an omniscient perspective (that of a storyteller who knows everyone's thoughts) and uses instead a first-person point of view. In this case Rudy Baylor, the soon-to-be law graduate, narrates events in the novel. In first-person point of view the story is seen only through the eyes of the narrator, not of any other character. Rudy narrates the story in present tense. This changed perspective enables Grisham to create a more fully developed picture of his protagonist. Readers get to know Rudy thoroughly, and we are invited to judge the extent to which Grisham's protagonist grows or changes, given his role in the events he describes. The present-tense narration also speeds the action of the novel. It conveys Rudy's ironic perspective and finely honed cynicism.

Some readers apparently didn't care for this technical shift in Grisham's writing. More than one librarian reported that people checked out

The Rainmaker only to return it unread the next day. Persistence pays off, however. Although *The Rainmaker* starts by gradually acquainting us with Rudy's humor instead of with rape, murder, suicide, explosion, or impending violence, in the long run it delivers an intriguing courtroom read.

CHARACTER DEVELOPMENT

In *The Rainmaker*, action and suspense are less important than the gradual unfolding of Rudy Baylor's character. For example, readers never have to wonder whether Rudy will survive his case against Great Benefit. Neither do readers have to worry much about whether the jury will return a verdict in favor of Rudy's client. Rudy acknowledges he was given everything he needed: facts, lucky breaks, a good judge and an evil but wealthy defendant. Moreover, except for a fight near novel's end, Rudy is never in physical danger.

Rudy Baylor is easily Grisham's most fully developed character. Although Adam Hall in *The Chamber* is also developed more fully than protagonists in the writer's earlier novels, we see Adam only from the outside as he struggles to make sense of his family's past. Rudy Baylor, on the other hand, tells readers a fair amount about himself while narrating the novel. At age 25 and with a well-developed sense of humor, Rudy explores the world around him and shows wit, sensitivity to ethical issues, and overall good sense.

Unlike Mitch McDeere in *The Firm*, a recent law school graduate who ranked at the top of his law class at an Ivy League school and is courted by numerous firms, Rudy falls somewhere in the crowd of his class at Memphis State—he lists his ranking as in the upper half (2)—and loses his first job before ever starting work. Although Mitch is "a rainmaker" (a superstar lawyer who earns plenty of money for his firm), Rudy can only dream of one day becoming one. And dream he does. Imagining himself bringing along a client worth $20 million when he joins Broadnax & Speer, Rudy muses, "I'd be an instant rainmaker, a bright young star with a golden touch. I might even ask for a larger office" (9).

Like Grisham's other heroes, Rudy lacks close family ties. His father is dead—no large loss, because his "decision to become a lawyer was irrevocably sealed when I realized my father hated the legal profession" (1). Rudy's mother has since been remarried, to a man named Hank with whom she tours the country in a Winnebago. Rudy observes that she "has no clue as to when I'll finish law school" (87).

Besides providing details about Rudy's biography, the first-person narration allows readers to see both the strengths and weaknesses of Rudy's character. On the positive side, Grisham shows his young attorney to be funny, wryly observant, ethical, kind, and smart. Rudy's humor is often dry and self-deprecating. When a potential client at the senior center purposely avoids Rudy and chooses another of Rudy's peers to provide him with free legal counsel, Rudy shrugs and observes, "Something tells me he will not be the last prospective client to go elsewhere for legal advice" (6). Rudy's talent for seeing beauty in the moment also frequently surfaces. When Miss Birdie Birdsong at last sits down with him for advice, he notes, "She leans forward, and I lean to my left, and at this precise moment as our heads come within inches of touching, I enter into my first conference as a legal counselor" (7). Although Rudy makes a pretense of being casual about such issues, ethics continually haunt him. He dreams of entering a profession that will enable him to improve social conditions, but, in law, he finds the opposite to be the case. Discouraged, he notes, "I've been reduced to a poacher in hospital cafeterias, for a thousand bucks a month. I'm sickened and saddened by what I've become, and I'm staggered by the speed at which I've fallen" (140). He worries about his unethical relationship with his paralegal, Deck (attorneys are not supposed to form partnerships with non-attorneys), about taping phone calls, about fair billing of clients, and about ambulance chasing. Rudy's friendship with Donny Ray shows that he thinks of his dying client as more than a potentially profitable court case. He invites Donny over to Miss Birdie's to spend the day, and he takes him to a baseball game. On a trip to gather evidence about Great Benefit, Rudy actively works on forgiving those who have wronged him: the attorney who tried to steal the Donny Ray Black case; even his former girlfriend, Sara Plankmore. Rudy's good sense and wisdom are often on display. Watching Leo Drummond, the lead attorney for the defense at a particularly vulnerable moment, Rudy acknowledges that Drummond is not responsible for what some "undetermined person" at Great Benefit has done to Donny Ray Black (234).

But Grisham also lets us see the flaws in Rudy's character. He alludes to potential difficulties with alcohol, emphasizes that Rudy has a problem controlling his temper, and repeatedly shows Rudy's narrow and negative views of women. The son of an alcoholic, Rudy refers to one of several "nasty bout[s] with cheap beer" (66). He mentions that one night he stopped drinking only when he started his shift as bartender at Yogi's. Because Rudy risks drinking too much, his hot temper is of special concern. When Rudy loses his new job at Broadnax & Speer, he smashes a bronze bust of "old man Broadnax" on his way out the door (34). Rudy repeatedly has violent thoughts. When Birdie Birdsong overworks him in the yard, he thinks he'd like to stuff her in a mulch bag (106). When on the sly Birdie opens his letter from the Tennessee Board of Law Examiners, notifying him that he has passed the bar exam, Rudy considers slapping the old woman in the face (182). At the law firm that tries to cheat him out of the Black case, Rudy pounds on the doors in a rage until a security guard escorts him away from the building (110–111). When Kelly Riker tells him about the beatings her husband has given her, Rudy dreams of bushwhacking the man with a baseball bat (156). He promises Kelly that if *his* daughter's husband beat her up, he'd "break his neck" (161).

Rudy's defense of the daughter he doesn't have and his desire for revenge in Kelly's case may seem surprising, given Rudy's otherwise negative attitude toward women. He describes one of his female classmates as "a real bitch [whom he suspects] wears a jockstrap" (4). When receptionists in a law office mistreat him during his job search, he imagines pretending to be the grieving husband of a woman killed by a heavily insured truck. Rudy ponders with great satisfaction, "It'd be hilarious to watch these snappy bitches spring from their seats, grinning wildly to get me some coffee" (70). Even when Rudy is pleased by the treatment he receives, he regards women as sexual objects. A receptionist who politely helps him has "a remarkable figure" and a "sultry" voice (121). Another is "cute" (271).

Characters supporting Rudy in *The Rainmaker* are humorously yet tenderly depicted. Birdie Birdsong, Deck Shifflet, and the Blacks have their weaknesses, but they have their beauty too. Birdie Birdsong genuinely cares about those she helps at Cypress Gardens. Through her, Rudy imagines what loneliness must be like; after Birdie is taken away by her children, Rudy wishes he had spent more time with her sipping her lukewarm coffee and watching television. Despite his unconventional legal practices, Rudy's law partner, Deck Shifflet, proves to be loyal and tireless. The Blacks, who bring suit against Great Benefit for failing to cover their son's bone marrow transplant, are gentle and trusting. Donny's mother speaks crudely, but she trusts the health-insurance system until it disappoints her, and she has faith that Rudy, despite his inexperience, will be able to help her family. Buddy Black, Donny Ray's

father, may spend hours drunk in his old Ford Fairlane, but before climb-
ing into the car he "sits with his son for a few minutes each morning,
usually leaves the room in tears, then tries to avoid everybody for the
rest of the day" (281). Grisham tells us little about Donny Ray Black
except that he has a twin brother. Donny Ray was living with his parents
when he became ill. Christlike in his suffering and patience, Donny Ray
weakens and dies before our eyes.

Rudy's antagonists in *The Rainmaker* are (1) the insurance company
goons whom Rudy interrogates during the trial, and (2) the lead attorney
for the defense, Leo Drummond, who uses unscrupulous tactics to defeat
Rudy in the courtroom. Compared with villains in Grisham's other novels, these antagonists are relatively invisible. They appear briefly in court
or in letters and memos, but Grisham does not develop them as characters. Greed seems to motivate the evil perpetrated by Great Benefit
employees. Besides greed, pride causes the attorneys representing Great
Benefit to commit illegal and unethical acts.

PLOT DEVELOPMENT

The Rainmaker's plot will be familiar to readers of *The Firm*. A young
or as yet untested attorney receives a great job offer but ends up on the
side of right, battling one or more corrupt organizations. Structured like
Grisham's other novels, *The Rainmaker* has more than 50 short chapters,
each broken into several brief scenes.

In *The Rainmaker*, Grisham doesn't use his standard method of creating
suspense—an initial terrifying, violent act that sets events in motion.
Instead, he uses Rudy's characterization (at least at first) to claim the
reader's attention. As the Black legal problem unfolds, however, suspense centers around Rudy's preparation for and litigation of their case.

Numerous subplots add humor and interest. Besides those mentioned
earlier, a process server driving a BMW hands Rudy a subpoena for
unpaid rent on his "grungy two-room efficiency" and for his outstanding
Texaco bills (36). Rudy's friend Booker must arrange an unofficial pardon
after Rudy in a pique destroys property at the law firm that fired him
before he even started work. Rudy's efforts to find employment, especially his appointments in the career counseling office at Memphis State,
will be poignantly familiar to anyone who has ever struggled to find a
job. When Rudy becomes a prime suspect in an arson case, he locates

for himself an attorney and an employer at the same time—a lawyer with mob connections appropriately named Bruiser Stone.

One of the most entertaining subplots involves the legal partnership that develops between Rudy and Deck Shiflett, his "paralawyer." Even though Deck can't pass the bar exam, he has plenty of practical skills and experience to pass on to Rudy, especially where signing up clients is concerned. Rudy accepts the instruction, eventually reciprocating with some legal lessons of his own.

Although Grisham doesn't begin *The Rainmaker* with an act of violence, that doesn't mean the novel lacks violence. A series of events involving Rudy's relationship with the battered housewife Kelly Riker happen just as his lawsuit against Great Benefit begins to unravel. At this point in the novel, suspense shifts in a surprising way and readers wonder how Rudy will reshape his career and perhaps his life in response to these unfortunate occurrences.

Reviewers—and even Grisham himself—have disagreed about Grisham's effectiveness in structuring *The Rainmaker's* plot. A review in the *Los Angeles Times* stated that "the complex plotting of *The Rainmaker* is Grisham's major accomplishment. From arson to bone marrow transplants to the fine print of insurance contracts, he seems to have thrown everything into this book. But the result isn't anarchic or confusing" (Abrahms BR8). The *Boston Globe* reviewer, on the other hand, criticized the novel, asking "why should [Grisham] care about shape, pace, momentum, tension, plausibility, literary distinction, even fundamental literacy," since he was almost certain to have another bestseller on his hands (Dyer "Rainmaker" 59:5)? Although Grisham himself likes the book and describes it as his funniest, even he acknowledges there is at least one scene he would "resequence" (Kelly "Not-So-Trying Times" 2D). An early version of the novel, more than 700 pages, was considerably longer than the finished text (424 pages). Although his favorite critic, his wife Renee, recommended he cut some material he loved— some "really funny lawyer stories that added nothing to the plot"— Grisham resisted. In the end, however, his editor at Doubleday agreed with Grisham's wife, "and most of what she didn't like is gone" (Kelly "Not-So-Trying Times" 2D). Although Grisham claimed in an interview in *USA Today* that Rudy's passion for Kelly in *The Rainmaker* is better than romances in his earlier novels, at least one reviewer disagreed, saying that "Rudy's romance with a 19-year-old battered wife has all the believability of a *Sweet Valley High* romance" (Donahue "Grisham Is Back" D1). Here the reviewer's comment probably makes sense, in that

Rudy and Kelly rarely talk and Rudy spends most of his energy fantasizing about Kelly's tanned legs. Typical of their conversations is one when Rudy is encouraging Kelly to file for divorce: Rudy says, "I'll help you get rid of this bum, and then we can have some fun" (303). Kelly doesn't show any more depth. Rudy notes she "likes to flirt, and she wants me to see her body" (162).

Although the novel is well plotted, Grisham leaves a couple of loose threads hanging. After indicating that Rudy probably didn't set fire to the Jonathan Lake offices, Grisham never lets readers know who did. Because the fire occurs shortly after an enraged Rudy tries to enter the building, the finger of suspicion points at him. A second loose thread was noted by a lawyer reviewing the novel for the *Houston Chronicle*. According to him, Grisham, who has Rudy show insurance manuals to Judge Kipler, should know that private conversations about a case between attorney and judge are "probably unethical in every state" (Drummond Z23).

Despite these objections to *The Rainmaker's* plot development, the *Boston Globe* reviewer acknowledged that the novel's courtroom drama is "fun to follow," especially insofar as it takes potshots at corporate greed. Even the novel's "inevitable ending" comes as a surprise (*Boston Globe* 61). The plot also has other positive elements. Grisham uses foreshadowing (dropping clues as to what will happen later in the novel) to heighten suspense. Moreover, none of his many references to alcohol and violence is gratuitous. The novel also contains an amusing intertextual reference to *The Firm*. At one point Rudy conjectures what he'd do if he won a large insurance case, acknowledging that "Me, I'd be off to the Caribbean with my one point three [million dollars], sailing my own ketch and sipping rum punch" (41).

THEMATIC ISSUES

It is easy to understand, given the present political climate, why *The Rainmaker* strikes a chord in so many American readers. Simultaneously idealistic and cynical, Rudy Baylor embodies many people's hopes for and frustration with big government, big business—in particular, medical insurance companies—and the legal justice system. Several characters in the novel besides Rudy Baylor feel angry and betrayed by the system. "They live on the economic margins and don't expect to ever do better. Others are [themselves] cynical manipulators of the system—guys in suits who know how to bend the rules and take somebody's last dime. The institutions are corrupt, incompetent or broke" (Abrahms BR8).

The Rainmaker may be autobiographical to the extent that Grisham presents through Rudy a second theme: Grisham's own disillusionment with the law. Certainly, the novel tracks Rudy's dissatisfaction with and doubts about his profession, which seems to him dirty and profit-mad. Part of Rudy Baylor's appeal, in fact, grows out of his status as "an American innocent," a person with ideals connected to an appreciation of democracy, who likes his shady employer even though Bruiser eventually goes on the lam to avoid prosecution. At least gangsters such as Bruiser are what they seem, unlike the Tinley, Britt attorneys and the Great Benefit insurance executives who commit illegal and immoral acts while pretending to be virtuous.

Effectively or not, the novel also argues for the power of love: both Rudy's for Kelly, and Dot and Buddy Black's for Donny Ray. Stripped of fortune and career by novel's end, Rudy has his priorities straight. They involve loving someone and contributing to society in a way that the practice of law prevents him from doing. Dot and Buddy's love for Donny Ray gives Dot, at least, strength to stand against a monolith, to demand justice from a system that will not provide it.

Finally, the novel presents a bleak portrait of health care in America. *The Rainmaker* poignantly states the problem: "So this is how the uninsured die. In a society filled with wealthy doctors and gleaming hospitals and state-of-the-art medical gadgetry and the bulk of the world's Nobel winners, it seems outrageous to allow Donny Ray Black to wither away and die without proper medical care" (261).

A READER-RESPONSE READING OF *THE RAINMAKER*

Reader-response criticism deals with how readers—either alone or in groups—receive texts, given the readers' class, gender, ethnicity, or sexual preference. Reader-response criticism has become increasingly popular in recent years in large part because of its association with postmodernism and feminist criticism, both of which emphasize the subjectivity of meaning and the importance of personal responses to literature and the effects gender has on how we read.

Reader-response critics tend to believe that "the work of literature is not an object separate from the reader; in a sense it does not exist until it is read. The reader's response is the most important part of the interpretive act" (Jacobus 13). Assuming this statement is true, a work's meanings may change from age to age, and these differing readings are a part of a literary work's history. Also, because each reader is unique, his or her responses to a novel are important and may shed new light on it. Always, "the reader supplies what the literary text omits, which can include the physical appearance of characters, the sensory experience of events, and a variety of unspoken background information, such as what it means to be male, female, young, old, sick, or well" (13).

If it weren't for my own recent experiences with illness, I would dismiss *The Rainmaker* as just another fun read. In earlier passes through the novel, I called it "fluff." I pitied the cancer victim, Donny Ray Black; enjoyed the courtroom victories of Rudy Baylor; and delighted in Grisham's humor. Although I realized the novel touched on an important contemporary issue—the state of health care in America—I focused in my early readings more on Rudy's lawyerly tactics to help his client than on the client's predicament.

This time, however, I'm reading *The Rainmaker* as part of writing this book while I am lying in a hospital bed in Chicago. Outside my window I can see waves rolling to shore on Lake Michigan. I am lucky to be here. It is November, and the excruciating pain I've been suffering since midsummer has just been diagnosed as chronic paroxysmal hemicrania, a rare form of vascular headache with only one known course of treatment. My doctor in Chicago has said he can help me, and already I am improving. I am a patient in the Diamond Headache Treatment Program at Columbus-Cabrini Medical Center. It has taken me a long time to get here, because the road to Chicago was blocked by my insurance company. It has insisted I receive treatment "in network," from local doctors in Dayton, Ohio, who are members of the insurance company's health-care consortium. As I lie in bed with *The Rainmaker*, I suddenly see the novel in a new way. It makes me realize how perilous my illness has been and affirms how frightening the state of health care is in the United States today.

Because popular fiction tends to exaggerate evil and good, it is easy to dismiss the importance of issues raised in *The Rainmaker*. There is little to like about Grisham's fictional Great Benefit Life, the company that refuses a life-saving bone marrow transplant to its cancer-stricken client; and the terminally ill Donny Ray Black seems saintly and, therefore, unreal. If you are healthy, you may be eager to distance yourself from events in the novel. You may regard Donny Ray as someone unlucky enough to have developed cancer, someone therefore unlike yourself.

Grisham helps us maintain that distance by giving Donny Ray comic/pathetic parents: a father who spends his days drunk in a rusted-out 1964 Ford Fairlane in his backyard, and a mother who obsesses about the "s'um bitches" at Great Benefit who are killing her son.

My own recent pain, however, forces me to see connections between Donny Ray's predicament and my own. Donny Ray's parents paid for health insurance coverage. According to their policy, Donny Ray is eligible to receive the bone marrow transplant he needs from his twin brother, Ron. I, too, have health insurance. As a professor at a state university, I am supposedly well protected by my insurance company. I always assumed I would receive the best possible treatment if something ever went wrong with me. Like Donny Ray's, my insurance policy is paid up fully.

As Jacobus says, my pain enables me to supply "what the literary text omits" (Jacobus 13), which in this case means I can more acutely imagine being sick while a blundering bureaucracy puts corporate policy in the way of my getting well. My experience enables me to empathize with Donny Ray. His illness, although life-threatening, is easier to treat than mine. He has leukemia, and doctors generally agree on a protocol for handling the disease. Donny Ray, they say, doesn't need to visit a distant clinic; he needs a bone marrow transplant that is available from his twin brother and in his hometown. The illness weakens Donny Ray while he awaits permission for treatment. Then the refusal letters start coming in, seven in all, including the letter calling Donny Ray's mother "stupid" when she presses the insurance company after it has denied her claim.

Reading *The Rainmaker* at this trying time in my own life helps me appreciate the frustrated efforts of Donny Ray's parents to help, and those of my own husband and younger son. Dot Black writes several times to the insurance company, asking them to review Donny Ray's files. She challenges their claims that Donny Ray is too old to receive coverage, that Donny Ray's leukemia is the result of a preexisting condition, that bone marrow transplants are excluded from the policy the Blacks hold. Dot also writes to her congressional representatives. She even tries, unsuccessfully, to enlist community support in getting help for her son. I myself am fortunate that my husband teaches in a medical school. He searches the literature on cluster and migraine headache and brings home medical articles that apply to my condition.

My Dayton neurologist prescribes a new drug for me; that doesn't work for Donny Ray Black because there are no alternative treatments. Deprived of the bone marrow transplant that could have saved him, Donny

Ray languishes in bed, weakens, and dies. Given the head pain I am feeling, I can imagine what his suffering must be like. I can imagine not feeling well enough to be angry. I can imagine the helplessness of having to rely on medical and insurance professionals who cannot or will not help.

My illness doesn't quite reach that point. I have money—not a lot, but enough so that, if necessary, I can pay my bills at the clinic in Chicago. Donny Ray doesn't have options. His procedure is prohibitively expensive at $175,000. Without insurance he is lost. And he is lost for no good reason. As Rudy learns through his research, a scam is in effect in 1991 at Great Benefit, the year Donny Ray needs a bone marrow transplant. As an experiment in keeping costs down, the insurance company has decided to automatically deny all claims because company researchers predict that only 1 in 25 of Great Benefit's clients is likely to sue if a claim is denied. Even if Great Benefit must go to court over 4 percent of their refusals, the company still ends up with greater profits than it would otherwise make. Surely real insurance companies aren't that cynical, cruel, and profit-hungry, we reason; and we continue reading *The Rainmaker*, perhaps feeling distanced from the action portrayed.

Even though my experience with my own insurer doesn't show evidence of insurance companies committing illegal acts, it does show them to be rigid, profit-driven, and unintentionally cruel. Spending my own money, I journey to Chicago where the headache specialist confirms I have chronic paroxysmal hemicrania, admits me to a hospital, and administers treatment. Before I can enter the hospital, however, my insurance company must give pre-approval. It refuses because I have "left the network" for treatment. Later, it will deny me the only treatment that works—because it is not listed as approved in its formulary (manual of approved medicines).

Thus, even though Donny Ray is unscrupulously denied a life-saving medical procedure, I see that in both Donny Ray's case and my own the medical decisions are being made not by physicians but by a largely nonmedical bureaucracy whose mandate is more to keep costs down than to cure. All these decisions are reached in the name of something called managed care. My insurance company—not my doctor—oversees my treatment, approves or disapproves the referrals my doctor makes, limits the length of time I can spend in the hospital, tells my doctors if their treatment of me is "wasteful," gives my doctors "guidelines" for treating me, and pays my doctors a flat fee for my medical care in an effort to keep that treatment to a minimum (*USA Today* "Patients Deserve to Know . . ." 12A).

Perhaps the most ironic aspect of my situation is that, indirectly, I am a part of the machine that prevents my receiving proper medical care. As a member of a women's investment club called Common Cents, a few months before my illness I voted with the group to buy a couple shares of the very insurance company that has harmed me with its cost-containing strategies. Also, as a writing consultant I have conducted workshops for employees of my insurance company in how to write letters that deny coverage!

Another irony is that Donny Ray Black and I could be considered the lucky ones. We both had insurance, and we both should have received help. For countless people in the United States, no medical care at all is within reach. In some cases Americans can't afford insurance; in others they are underinsured, receiving care only in narrowly prescribed situations, none of which include preventive screenings such as those for cancer, none of which cover routine office visits and tests. Surely, in telling the story of Donny Ray Black, Grisham wants us to see the dark and frightening implications for all of us of Donny's case.

Reader criticism, such as what you have just read, ensures we do so. It requires readers to entwine their own life stories around the ones they read about. It asserts the importance of biographical events in each reader's life. Our real lives nearly merge with the fictional lives we read about, as writer and readers together create meaning from a work of art.

The Runaway Jury
(1996)

As this book headed to press, John Grisham published his seventh novel, *The Runaway Jury*. It concerns a multi-million dollar lawsuit brought by Celeste Wood, the widow of a smoker in Biloxi, Mississippi, against a large tobacco company, Pynex. Her husband, Jacob L. Wood, died at age 51 after having smoked three packs of cigarettes a day for more than thirty years. Should the widow be compensated for her loss or was Wood's death "simply the result of choices he freely made?" (Donahue 1D).

In *The Runaway Jury*, Grisham focuses not on victims or attorneys as he has in earlier novels; instead, he zeros in on the jury hearing the case and in particular, on the actions of its most enigmatic member, Nicholas Easter, and on those of Nicholas's off-jury partner, Marlee. Although readers are introduced to these two characters at the beginning of the novel, not until the end do we learn what motivates Nicholas's and Marlee's actions.

Besides developing an intriguing plot, Grisham provides a great deal of information about jury selection and conduct in *The Runaway Jury*. In the book's early chapters, he describes the tobacco defense; a consortium of three other companies besides Pynex working to ensure that a jury sympathetic to its interests get selected and that a verdict in favor of tobacco gets rendered. In addition to the usual questionnaires that prospective jurors complete, attorneys representing tobacco interests, especially "a pudgy thug named [Rankin] Fitch," have reconnaissance photography and the notes of private detectives to help them decide who among the prospective jurors would likely side with the tobacco industry and who with the plaintiff. The plaintiff's lawyers have access to similar information and use it as shamelessly to achieve their own ends. "Grisham describes all . . . [this] without indignation, level reporting of the facts being his constant narrative demeanour. . . . As was demonstrated in the OJ Simpson case, such jury-fixing is legal and has almost become the most important part of the trial, although it seems to make a nonsense of justice" (Sexton 34).

Worse, however, is that once the jury gets selected, the defense lawyers begin a "frankly criminal effort" to secure a decision in tobacco's favor (Sexton 34). They stop at nothing to sway the jury's minds: threatening to reveal information about a secret abortion to a female juror's husband, making the spouse of another juror think the FBI is about to arrest him, and threatening the job of still another juror by buying up the grocery chain that employs him.

Were it not for Nicholas Easter, the Wood trial would have ended as had all the others Grisham mentions: with an easy victory for tobacco. Nicholas Easter, however, has legal savvy and leadership skills, both of which he uses to counter tobacco's efforts. Having finagled his way onto the jury, he wins the confidence of other jury members by insisting, among other things, that the jury's meals be served on real dishes and eaten with real silver. More importantly, his control over jury members and ultimately his control over the outcome of the trial is revealed to attorneys on both sides through his off-jury colleague Marlee. She lets Fitch and his tobacco cohorts know in advance that juror Jerry Fernandez will carry a *Sports Illustrated* into the courtroom, what Nicholas Easter will wear to court, and that the jury will one day do the pledge of allegiance in unison before court convenes.

Convinced that Marlee can deliver a verdict in tobacco's favor, Fitch agrees to pay her $10 million for it. To heighten suspense, Fitch's henchmen race to uncover the motives behind Nicholas's and Marlee's actions, learning after the money is already in Marlee's hands the secret she has successfully hidden. Once Marlee has the cash, Nicholas convinces the jury to rule in favor of the widow and to see that she is generously compensated for the loss of her husband. Unlike Mitch McDeere in *The Firm* who keeps the bad guys' money, Marlee and Nicholas only *borrow* tobacco's $10 million, investing it in the stock market based on what they know will happen when the verdict is in. Once they amass their own fortune, they return Fitch's $10 million to him.

According to Grisham, he based the novel on a real trial held several years ago in rural Mississippi, the plaintiff widowed by a man who smoked four packs a day. "The tobacco company won the case," Grisham said, "but there were lots of stories . . . about the investigation of the jury prior to trial and about manipulation of the jurors during trial" (Kelly 9D). Besides his familiarity with this real smoking trial, Grisham shows in *The Runaway Jury* an understanding of the total smoking controversy as recently described in the following nonfiction works: *Ashes to Ashes: America's Hundred-Year Cigarette War, The Public Health*, and *The Unabashed Triumph of Philip Morris*. Tobacco experts in Grisham's novel present the evidence at trial from a variety of viewpoints—biochemical, statistical, and epidemiological.

So far, *The Runaway Jury* promises to sell as well or better than Grisham's other thrillers. Doubleday did a 2.8 million copy printing of the novel and sold more than 500,000 books within the first month. These statistics make it "the fastest-selling Grisham book ever" (Weeks C01). One reason for its success may be the pleasure Grisham took in writing it. He delighted, he said, in deciding how attorneys could co-opt a jury. His lawyers offer pay-offs to jurors, threaten to reveal jurors' secrets, and seek out weak juror marriages to compromise. Equally fascinating to Grisham is the possibility that cigarette manufacturers could be successfully sued by those who smoke their product.

One might wonder, given Grisham's thorough presentation of the legal issues surrounding cigarette liability and given his biased coverage, whether he fears reprisal from the cigarette industry. He claims he does not. In a *USA Today* interview, Grisham says he expected a response from the insurance industry after publication of *The Rainmaker*, but he heard nothing. He's guessing the tobacco industry will react similarly. "You know, it's easy for them to say, look, this is just a work of fiction and that's it" (Kelly 9D). Harmless, in other words.

Harmless or not, the novel was popular with reviewers. It received more praise than did any of his earlier efforts. *Publishers Weekly* describes *The Runaway Jury* as Grisham's "most rewarding novel to date," in that it deals with "arguments of genuine pith [that] are hammered out and resolved in a manner that is both intellectually and emotionally satisfying" (72). The *New York Times* and the *Boston Globe* concur, the *Times* adding that the novel's "eventual outcome is far more entertainingly unpredictable than anything Mr. Grisham has done before" (C20), *The Globe* calling the novel "an exceptionally powerful fantasy" (57). The *Chicago Tribune* says *The Runaway Jury* is "Grisham's best storytelling to date," citing as its strengths Grisham's timing and "high-powered narration" (N3). The *Los Angeles Times* credits Grisham for his journalistic expertise that is both "comprehensive" and "evenhanded" (E3). The *Christian Science Monitor* says, "John Grisham's latest legal thriller . . . has it all: mystery, legal maneuvering, behind-the-scenes views of a trial, jury tampering, and plenty of other skullduggery" (B4).

A few reviews were less positive. *Time* concludes the novel is "claustrophobic and actionless, woefully deficient in gun fights and car chases" (85). Despite having praised Grisham's journalistic expertise, the *Los Angeles Times* labels *The Runaway Jury* a "peculiar novel, as bestsellers go. It has almost no sex, no violence, [and] no character with an interesting interior life" (E3).

CHARACTERIZATION AND SETTING

As the *Los Angeles Times* review indicates, characterization in *The Runaway Jury* is extremely thin, but undeveloped characters are probably a necessity given the story Grisham tells. The real identities of Nicholas Easter and his cohort, Marlee, are crucial to plot, so readers are kept in the dark until the novel's final pages about Nicholas and Marlee and their motivations. Descriptions of the two are sketchily drawn. In chapter one, readers see Nicholas Easter through a hidden camera. There is nothing unusual about his appearance. Unsettling to those spying on him is the inconclusiveness of the information they have gathered: he is a part-time student, but they are unable to turn up information about where he studied, how long he was a student, what he majored in, and whether his grades were any good. Marlee, Nicholas's partner, is similarly nondescript. With short brown hair and brown eyes, "she looked great in anything or nothing, really, but for the moment she wanted no one to notice her" (59). A final look at Marlee, when she appears before Fitch in a Dupont Circle Indian restaurant, dropping "in from nowhere, just appear[ing] like an angel," maintains much of her mystery (399). Grisham's arch-evil attorney Rankin Fitch also remains one dimensional. Readers know only that he is driven by power and profit as are most antagonists in Grisham's novels.

Setting is also skimpily treated. The story takes place in Biloxi, Mississippi, with Grisham mostly ignoring that fact. Although the film version of the novel will no doubt offer a corrective, there is scant reference to the setting except for a water side resort meeting of assorted tobacco company representatives, a jurors' trip to the French Quarter, and a fishing trip. Marlee's journey to New Orleans in connection with the trial might as well have been to Peoria or Ft. Kearney. Even the searches by those hoping to learn Nicholas's and Marlee's correct identities, one requiring a trip to Gardner, Texas, involve more research than setting.

SOCIAL/HISTORICAL ISSUES

The Runaway Jury deals with two important social issues, the first of which is tobacco litigation. The novel comes at a good time: as the public grows more and more aware of the dangers of using tobacco. Not only that, but in New Orleans a real court recently rejected a huge class action suit brought by millions of smokers. So far, tobacco remains unbeaten. "Every year the suspense builds. Can Big Tobacco's money and political clout hold out forever against the moral consensus that has developed against it?" (Harris E3).

Grisham's idea for the novel—how one or two people might thwart the efforts of tobacco money to protect its interests in the courtroom—will intrigue anyone concerned with how a product as dangerous as tobacco continues to be sold in the United States and how efforts to sue tobacco companies for the illnesses they cause have been unsuccessful. Early chapters provide background. Four conglomerates, all of which can trace their origins back to nineteenth-century tobacco brokers, send representatives to approve the expenditure of pooled money to fight the Wood lawsuit in Mississippi. These four companies manufactured ninety-eight percent of all cigarettes sold in the United States and Canada. The money pooled by this group is known as The Fund. It is highly secret and used for "hardball tactics in lawsuits; to hire the best and meanest defense lawyers, the smoothest experts, the most sophisticated jury consultants" (10). When Rankin Fitch looked into the matter, he found the Wood case against Pynex was the fifty-fifth such suit. Even so, "Not one penny had ever been paid to a plaintiff in a cigarette case" (16).

In creating his courtroom scenes, Grisham displays his thorough research and knowledge of the issues surrounding tobacco. At base, the plaintiff contends that tobacco companies should not escape liability for continuing to sell a product known to be addictive and dangerous even when "properly" used. The defense argues otherwise: that a smoker assumes the risk when he or she continues to smoke despite cigarettes' "widely publicized hazards" (Stubbs 10B). The plaintiff's response—that tobacco companies willfully manipulate the amounts of nicotine in their product to ensure smokers' addiction and that many smokers become addicted as teenagers, before they are capable of making informed decisions—while persuasive this response continues not to yield a plaintiff victory in real life.

Grisham invents numerous experts to testify for the plaintiff and to educate readers about the dangers of smoking. The first is the deceased Jacob Wood who describes in a videotaped deposition his smoking history and unsuccessful efforts to break the habit. Jurors can see his wan form as he speaks: "He was thin, gaunt, and pale, and took oxygen from a tiny tube running from behind his bony neck into his nose" (57). A second witness, Dr. Milton Fricke, presents details about the effects, chemical and pharmacological, of tobacco smoke on the human body. According to him, about 10% of cigarette smokers eventually contract lung cancer. How tobacco injures the body is the area of expertise of Grisham's next plaintiff's witness. Dr. Robert Bronsky uses extensive graphics to show that tobacco has more than 4000 compounds, including "16 known carcinogens, 14 alkalis, and numerous other compounds with known biological activity" (83). Comprised of tiny drops of gases, tobacco smoke enters smokers' lungs when they inhale with about 50% of the smoke being retained. Dr. Bronsky also discusses nicotine, showing how it constricts superficial vessels in arms and legs, raises blood pressure, increases the smoker's pulse, and makes the heart beat harder. "He made a single cigarette sound like a dose of lethal poison" (85). Dr. Bronsky also covers the "irritants" in tobacco smoke: ammonia, volatile acids, aldehydes, phenols, and ketones. Although these irritants stimulate secretion of mucus, they delay mucus removal by slowing the work of cilia in the bronchial tubes (90). Grisham's expert witnesses also present the statistical probabilities of developing lung cancer. According to Dr. Hilo Kilvan, a person who smokes fifteen cigarettes a day for ten years is at ten times greater risk than a person who doesn't smoke. Kilvan indicates cigarettes are responsible for the deaths of 400,000 Americans annually—and that's assuming they are used properly. "They are deadly if used exactly as intended!"(129). In addition to these experts, Grisham has an animal researcher, Dr. James Ueuker, testify for the plaintiff. Ueker's testimony (that animal research affirms the data of other studies) gets cut short because several jurors are pained at the thought of smoking tests being performed on rabbits and beagles.

Perhaps most frightening is evidence an expert presents that cigarette manufacturers callously manipulate levels of nicotine to ensure smokers' addiction. Lawrence Krigler, once employed by Pynex, testifies that he developed a low nicotine strain of tobacco only to have the company discredit his work. As he reports on the stand, the reason the company, then called U-Tab, discredited him was that they "could not afford to produce a leaf with markedly lower nicotine, because nicotine meant profits. [In other words], the industry had known since the late thirties that nicotine was physically addictive" (168). When Krigler completes his testimony, he has reason to fear for his life. He is escorted by private plane back to Florida where a tobacco exposé that he has written will be published if he dies an untimely death.

A former Surgeon General establishes that cigarette companies target young people, as well as both sexes and different social groups, hoping to get them to smoke. In their ads, tobacco companies make smoking look "fun, sophisticated, even healthy . . . They advertise and promote like mad, but when one of their customers dies from lung cancer they claim the person should have known better" (191).

Final plaintiff's testimony comes from three sources: Leon Robilio, a cancer victim lacking a larynx; Dr. Art Kallison, who puts a dollar value on Jacob Wood's life; and Wood's widow, Celeste. Robilio testifies in a raspy voice with a microphone held close to his throat, how he once worked as a pro-tobacco activist in Washington. His biggest sin, he admits, was denying that tobacco companies target young people with their advertising. Art Allison values Jacob Wood's lost earnings at $835,000. He assures the jury, however, that he can't place a monetary value on the rest of Wood's life. His calculations "had nothing to do with the pain and suffering Mr. Wood endured as he died; had nothing to do with the loss his family had endured" (244–45). Celeste Wood, the last witness, talks about her happy life with Jacob, about their children and grandchildren, and finally about their thwarted plans for the future, due to the cancer the cigarettes caused.

That Grisham sides with the plaintiff's case is made clear by the way he presents the defense. Before letting the defense's first witness, D. Martin Jankle, CEO of Pynex, testify, Grisham establishes that the man is an alcoholic. Sober the day he testifies, Jankle emphasizes that people exercise free choice when they smoke. Outlining the various brands of cigarettes that his company produces and showing their differing levels of tar and nicotine, Jankle says, "Pynex allowed each consumer to decide how much tar and nicotine he or she wanted. Choice. Choice. Choice. Choose the level of tar and nicotine. Choose the number of cigarettes you smoke each day. Choose whether or not to inhale. Make the intelligent choice of what you do to your body with cigarettes" (270). Dr. Denise McQuade, the second witness for the defense, argues that cigarette advertising is no different from any other kind and that ads are an integral part of our culture. She cites McDonalds' advertising, arguing that here is a company promoting unhealthful eating habits for our children. "Do we sue them because our kids are fatter?" because McDonalds uses "dubious advertising practices" (294)?

Based on interviews with jurors in earlier tobacco cases, the defense decides not to raise the issue of nicotine addiction. Despite all the fancy theories and evidence offered to suggest that tobacco isn't addictive, "everyone knew the opposite to be true. It was that simple" (306). Thus, a Dr. Gunther is called to "muddy" plaintiff testimony, arguing that no one can be sure whether or not cigarettes cause cancer. Needing research to bolster their opinions, the defense attorneys call a Dr. Olney, who claims he has tried to induce cancer in mice but has been unsuccessful. With that the defense rests its case.

In writing *The Runaway Jury*, Grisham has performed an important service, especially for young people who have not yet started smoking or who have experimented only casually with tobacco. It is hard to read this novel without becoming educated about the dangers of smoking and without profoundly fearing the consequences of tobacco use.

The second issue that Grisham tackles is American jurisprudence itself, in particular our faith in juries as the principle means of achieving justice. Many Americans recall their discomfort "over what the Simpson trial revealed about the arcane science of jury selection" (Harris E3). Consultants could legally put together a jury sympathetic to the prosecution or the defense, but by doing so they violate the principle that a jury ought to be twelve ordinary citizens randomly selected for service.

But randomly selected they are not in *The Runaway Jury*, nor do they measure up to our idealized notions of what a jury should be or do. Besides having been selected based on experts' opinions of which side they will support, jurors in the Wood trial are depicted by Grisham as woefully vulnerable to influence. "Every jury has a leader and that's where you find your verdict" (11). This piece of Grisham wisdom tells us all we need to know about the fragility of most people's opinions; a jury can be no stronger than the individuals serving on it. If the motives of the leader are suspect, then justice can only accidentally be served. From the earliest moments of the Wood trial, Grisham shows readers that Nicholas Easter is in charge of the jury. Although Herman Grimes is chosen foreperson, there is evidence Nicholas Easter is responsible for that selection. Grimes is blind and Easter sees that he becomes Grimes's guide and translator. Easter works behind the scenes in other ways, ensuring the jury gets treated well, speaking for the jury with the judge, and systematically becoming friends with the other jurors.

Grisham also shows how each member of the jury is vulnerable in some way and that attorneys for either side can capitalize on this vulnerability. Before the Wood trial even begins, tobacco attorneys have begun to locate these Achilles heels. In the case of one juror, they even create a scam and entice her husband into becoming involved.

In *The Runaway Jury* Grisham depicts attorneys on both sides as power hungry and greedy, out to extract a verdict from the jury at any price. Even if attorneys know they have "right" on their side in a case, is it proper for them to tamper with a jury?

THEMATIC ISSUES

For a novel to express a persuasive theme, it needs powerful characters for readers to identify with. Grisham's *The Runaway Jury* has neither. Themes grow out of fictionalized human struggles against mighty forces: a diety, nature, or strong human adversaries. In *The Runaway Jury* Nicholas's and Marlee's characterizations and motives are so obscure and Grisham's focus so starkly on the issues surrounding tobacco litigation, that thematic threads are barely discernible in the fabric of the tale. Not without reason, numerous reviewers use the words "journalistic" and "documentary" to describe Grisham technique in this seventh novel. What they mean is that the novel's content nearly lacks a human frame. Grisham lets us know what goes on behind the scenes at the Wood trial—and, by extension, at real trials—but he doesn't make us feel tangled in the action. For readers to personalize the events in fiction and for fiction to teach us lessons, we need to be able to merge our lives, even briefly, with characters in the fictional world.

Still, if one places *The Runaway Jury* in context with Grisham's other novels, one can see similarities between the Nicholas-Marlee team and Grisham's other protagonists whom he develops more fully. Nicholas and Marlee, as one dimensional as they are, resemble Rudy Baylor in *The Rainmaker* and Grisham's earlier heroes who "show . . . up the stupidity and wickedness of the big guns and win" (Walter T16). As readers we appreciate being reassured that no evil force is too powerful to withstand the little guy who is right. At one point in *The Runaway Jury*, Nicholas Easter says his fellow jurors are the trial's most important people; thanks to him, those "important people" reach the correct verdict. Readers, meanwhile, feel affirmed by the jury's actions. After all, don't we want to hear "that ordinary people can easily outwit blind power, despite all its blizzards of paperwork and surveillance cameras and bribes and schemes and threats?" (Walter T16). If *The Runaway Jury* manages to convey a theme, that is it.

Bibliography

WORKS BY JOHN GRISHAM

A Time to Kill. New York: Bantam Doubleday Dell, 1989.
The Chamber. New York: Doubleday, 1994.
The Client. New York: Bantam Doubleday Dell, 1993.
The Firm. New York: Bantam Doubleday Dell, 1991.
The Pelican Brief. New York: Bantam Doubleday Dell, 1992.
The Rainmaker. New York: Doubleday, 1995.
The Runaway Jury. New York: Doubleday, 1996.

WORKS ABOUT JOHN GRISHAM

"A League of His Own." *USA Today* 1 July 1994: Weekend 4.
Bearden, Michelle. "John Grisham." *Publishers Weekly* 22 Feb. 1993: 70–71.
Conroy, Sarah Booth. "The Tort Story Writer." *Washington Post* 28 Mar. 1992: C1–C6.
Current Biography Yearbook 1993. New York: H. W. Wilson, 1993, pp. 221–224.
Donahue, Diedre. "Grisham's Law: Thrills Sell." *USA Today* 4 Mar. 1993: D1.
Duffy, Martha. "Grisham's Law." *Time* 8 May 1995: 87.
"First, Let's Top-Bill All the Lawyers." *Los Angeles Times* 28 August 1994: 26.

Freedland, Jonathan. "The Law Lord." *Guardian* 30 May 1994: 2:2–3.

Gillers, Stephen. "Grisham's Law." *Nation* 18 Apr. 1994: 509.

Hendersen, Cliff. "Mr. Clean." *TWA Ambassador* Aug. 1995: 31–33.

Hubbard, Kim. *People* 16 Mar. 1992: 43–44.

Kaufman, Joanne. "Law and the Author: Grisham's Next Case." *Wall Street Journal* 10 Mar. 1992: A 16.

Kelly, Katy. "Grisham Suits Up to Try One Last Case." *USA Today* 14 Apr. 1995: D1.

———. "Not-So-Trying Times for John Grisham." *USA Today* 17 Apr. 1995: 1D–2D.

Martelle, Scott. "Hot on the Case." *Detroit News* 3 Mar. 1993: C1.

Mathews, Tom. "Book 'Em." *Newsweek* 15 Mar. 1993: 78–81.

O'Briant, Don. "Schools Urge Students to Pick Up a Best Seller." *Atlanta Constitution* 16 June 1994: D1.

———. "Grisham to Run Southern Magazine." *Atlanta Constitution* 16 Aug. 1994: B6.

Oldenberg, Ann. "He's Keeping Cool Despite Sizzling Sales." *USA Today* 2 June 1994: 1.

Scherer, Ron. "Grisham, Crichton Books Serve as a Boarding Pass." *Christian Science Monitor* 2 Sept. 1993: 14:1.

Skube, Michael. "Taste and Judgment Are Odd Companions." *Atlanta Journal Constitution* 18 Apr. 1993: N10.

Stark, Steven. "The Lawyer as Hero." *Boston Globe* 19 Apr. 1993: 15:1.

Street, Robin. "The Grisham Brief." *Writer's Digest* July 1993: 32–34.

Streitfeld, David. "Hot Hot Hot! What's He Got? John Grisham's Megaseller Mystique." *Washington Post* 30 June 1993: D1.

"Summer Reading for the CEO." *USA Today* 12 July 1993: B3:12.

USA Today. "Grisham." 30 June 1992: D5.

Welkos, Robert. "A Novel Success Story." *Los Angeles Times* 19 Oct. 1992: F.

Will, Ed. "Best Seller No Threat to Anonymity." *Denver Post* 2 Apr. 1992: F1:5.

REVIEWS AND CRITICISM

The Firm

Bernikow, Louise. *Cosmopolitan* Apr. 1991: 40.

Kennedy, Pagan. *Village Voice* 9 July 1991: S7.

Lane, Anthony. "Current Cinema: 'Against the Law.'" *New Yorker* 27 Dec. 1993: 148–52.

Lee, James Ward. "Attorney Learns about the Wrong Side of the Law." *Houston Post* 7 July 1991: C5.

Prescott, Peter. "Murky Maneuvers in a Lethal Law Firm." *Newsweek* 25 Feb. 1991: 63.

Selvin, Joel. "Legal Eagle Turns Snoop for the FBI." *San Francisco Chronicle* 21 Feb. 1991: E5.

Stasio, Marilyn. "Crime." *New York Times* 24 Mar. 1991: 7.

Winks, Robin W. "Old Thriller Formulas Still Work." *Boston Sunday Globe* 31 May 1992: 96.

The Pelican Brief

Bennett, Elizabeth. "Getting a 'Firm' Grip on Success." *Houston Post* 10 May 1992: C5.

Clay, Lawrence. "Supreme Court Murders Lead to Suspenseful Chase." *Denver Post* 22 Mar. 1992: E6:2.

Drabelle, Dennis. "Grisham's 'Pelican Brief' Doesn't Quite Fly." *USA Today* 5 Mar. 1992: D6.

Dyer, Richard. "Grisham's 'Pelican Brief': A Rehash of White Collar Crooks." *Boston Globe* 10 Mar. 1992: 56:3.

Hawtree, Christopher. "Thoroughly Modern Thriller." *Spectator* 1 Aug. 1992: 30.

Lehmann-Haupt, Christopher. "2 Justices Are Dead. Who Profits?" *New York Times* 27 Feb. 1992: C22.

"Not for the Birds." *Forbes* 30 Aug. 1993: 24.

O'Briant, Don. "Grisham's New Thriller Entertains." *Atlanta Journal* 8 Mar. 1992: N8.

Olson, Ray. "Adult Fiction: 'The Pelican Brief' by John Grisham." *Booklist* 15 Jan. 1992: 883.

Press, Aric. "A Breech of Contract." *Newsweek* 16 Mar. 1992: 73.

Pugh, Clifford. " 'Pelican Brief' a Soft Follow-Up to 'The Firm.' " *Houston Post* 23 Feb. 1992: 6:4.

Skow, John. "Legal Eagle." *Time* 9 Mar. 1992: 70.

Toobin, Jeffrey. "Still More Lawyer Bashing from Novelist John Grisham." *Chicago Tribune* 23 Feb. 1992: 14:4.

The Client

Colbert, James. "Grisham's Latest: Passing Judgment on 'The Client.' " *Chicago Tribune* 28 Feb. 1993: 14:7.

Coughlin, Ruth. "A Chase Novel Not Really Worth Pursuing." *Detroit News* 3 Mar. 1993: C1.

Dyer, Richard. "Grisham Back on Track in 'Client.' " *Boston Globe* 10 Mar. 1993: 49.

Goodrich, Lawrence. "Topical Legal Thriller Spins an Intriguing But Improbable Tale." *Christian Science Monitor* 5 Mar. 1993: 10.

Holt, Patricia. "Boy Has Key to Mob Hit in Grisham Thriller." *San Francisco Chronicle* 4 Mar. 1993: E5.

Larson, Susan. "A Small Child Shall Lead Them." *New Orleans Times-Picayune* 7 Mar. 1993: E7.

Pugh, Clifford. "Grisham's New Mystery: A Missing Plot." *Houston Post* 21 Mar. 1993: C4.

The Chamber

Andig, Bettye. "Death Watch." *New Orleans Times-Picayune* 15 May 1994: E6:5.

Cook, Bruce. "John Grisham Attempts a Different Kind of Legal Thriller." *Chicago Tribune* 26 June 1994: 14:3.

Coughlin, Ruth. "Chamber." *Detroit News* 25 May 1994: 3.

Donahue, Diedre. "Grisham's Latest Puts Death Penalty on Trial." *USA Today* 27 May 1994: D1.

Dyer, Richard. "Grisly 'Chamber' Departs from Grisham Formula." *Boston Globe* 28 June 1994: 53.

Goodman, Walter. "Getting to Know Grandpa under Penalty of Death." *New York Times* 29 July 1994: C27.

Goodrich, Lawrence. "A Race Against a Mississippi Execution." *Christian Science Monitor* 10 June 1994: 14.

Hartman, Diane. "New Grisham Thriller Different But Absorbing." *Denver Post* 22 May 1994: E8:2.

Magee, David. "Grisham's Latest Novel Sets Record." *New Orleans Times-Picayune* 29 May 1994: A35.

Mauro, Tony. " 'The Chamber': Fiction Offers Look at Reality." *USA Today* 3 Aug. 1994: 3A.

O'Rourke, Andrew. "Grisham's 'The Chamber' Is Loaded with Missed Potential." *Atlanta Constitution* 26 May 1994: C27.

Parks, Louis. "Grisham on a Slow Simmer." *Houston Chronicle* 3 July 1994: Z18, Z22.

People. "Rev. of 'The Chamber.' " Vol. 41 no. 24: 26.

Publishers Weekly. "Rev. of 'The Chamber.' " Vol. 24 no. 22: 37.

The Rainmaker

Abrahms, Garry. "There's Outlaws, and Then There's Bad Guys." *Los Angeles Times* 14 May 1995: BR8.

Boston Globe. 14 May 1995: BR8.

Bruni, Frank. "Verdict Is Positive on the 'Rainmaker,' a Lower-Key Grisham." *Detroit News and Free Press* 30 Apr. 1995: J8.

Cerio, Gregory. "John Grisham." *People Weekly* 8 May 1995: 151.

Donahue, Diedre. "Grisham Is Back on Firm Ground." *USA Today* 12 Apr. 1995: D1.

Drummond, Jeff. "Grisham's New-Found Humor Makes 'The Rainmaker' an Enjoyable Read." *Houston Chronicle* 14 May 1995: Z23.

Dyer, Richard. " 'Rainmaker': Grisham Washes Out." *Boston Globe* 22 June 1995: 59 and 61.

Holt, Patricia. "Grisham Is Back in Court." *San Francisco Chronicle* 13 Apr. 1995: D1.

Kakutani, Michiko. "Chasing Ambulances before Dreams." *New York Times* 28 Apr. 1995: 33:1.

Nolan, Tom. "Grisham Back in Form." *Wall Street Journal* 27 Apr. 1995: A12.

USA Today. "Patients Deserve to Know Doctors' Financial Deals." 28 Nov. 1995: 12A.

The Runaway Jury

Donahue, Diedre. "Grisham's 'Jury' Leaves Reasonable Doubts." *USA Today* 15 May 1996: 1D.

Dyer, Richard. "The Runaway Jury." *Boston Globe* 29 May 1996: 57.

Goodrich, Lawrence J. "A Jury of One's Peers Goes Up in Smoke." *Christian Science Monitor* 27 June 1996: B4.

Harris, Michael. "Book Review/Novel; Four Tobacco Firms, a Lawsuit and a Stalker." *Los Angeles Times* 3 June 1996: E3.

Kelly, Katy. "Grisham's Smoking Gun: 'Runaway Jury' Paints Picture of Devious Tobacco Industry." *USA Today* 29 May 1996: 9D.

Lehmann-Haupt, Christopher. "In a Legal Thriller, Big Tobacco on the Defensive." *New York Times* 23 May 1996: 20C.

Petrakos, Chris. "Holy Smoke—'Runaway Jury' Is Grisham at His Best." *Chicago Tribune* 4 June 1996: 3N.

Publishers Weekly "The Runaway Jury." Vol. 243 no. 19: 72.

Sexton, David. "Twelve Greedy Men." *The Spectator* 18 May 1996: 34.

Skow, John. "The Runaway Plot Line." *Time* 85.

Stubbs, A. Thomas. " 'Runaway Jury' Deserves to be Runaway Success." *Atlanta Journal and Constitution* 21 May 1996: 10B.

Walter, Natasha. "Worms that Turn up Millions." *The Guardian* 3 May 1996: T16.

Weeks, Linton. "The 'Runaway' Bestseller; Grisham and His New Book a Winning Team at Convention." *Washington Post* 17 June 1996: C01.

WORKS ABOUT GRISHAM NOVELS MADE INTO FILMS

"Author Likes Film Version of Best-Seller." *Houston Chronicle* 30 June 1993: 5D.
DeTurenne, Veronique. "Stars, Fans Turn Out for 'Firm' Premiere." *Los Angeles Daily News* 30 June 1993: 2D.
Eller, Claudia. "Movie Deal on Unwritten Grisham Book Sets Record." *Los Angeles Times* 17 July 1993: A23.
"First Let's Top Bill the Lawyers." *Los Angeles Times* 28 Aug. 1994: 2C.
Franklin, Daniel. " 'The Client' Breeds Anarchy." *Atlanta Constitution* 4 Aug. 1994: A15.
Larson, Susan. "Bumpy Flight." *New Orleans Times-Picayune* 1 Mar. 1992: E6.
Maslin, Janet. "One Part Grisham, Three Parts Telling Detail." *New York Times* 20 July 1994: C11.
Pope, John. "Roberts Gives Pelican Briefing." *New Orleans Times-Picayune* 21 May 1993: A17.
Turan, Kenneth. "The Firm of Julia, Denzel, Grisham & Pakula." *Los Angeles Times* 17 Dec. 1993: F1.

WORKS ABOUT LAWYERS AND THRILLERS

Fein, Esther. "Forget Those Legal Briefs: Novels by Lawyers Pay Off." *New York Times* 20 July 1992: D6.
Kaufman, Joanne. "Legions of Lawyers Turned Novelists." *Wall Street Journal* 1 Aug. 1991: A10.
Klinkenborg, Verlyn. "Law's Labors Lost: The Lawyer as Hero and Anti-Hero." *New Republic* 14 Mar. 1994: 32–38.
Torry, Saundra. "For Lawyers, Writing Can Be a Novel Experience—and Escape." *Washington Post* 17 Feb. 1992: WBIZ 5:1.

BOOKS ON CRIME FICTION

Baker, Robert A., and Michael T. Nietzel. *Private Eyes: One Hundred and One Knights—A Survey of American Detective Fiction 1922–1984.* Bowling Green: Bowling Green State University Press, 1985.
Nevins, Francis M. "Law School Seminar on Popular Fiction and Film." *Murder*

Is Academic: The Teaching and Criticism of Crime Fiction on Campus. Vol. 3 (November 1995): 1–3.

Palmer, Jerry. "The Thriller." *Whodunit? A Guide to Crime, Suspense and Spy Fiction*, ed. H.R.F. Keating. New York: Van Nostrand Reinhold, 1982.

———. *Thrillers: Genesis and Structure of a Popular Genre*. New York: St. Martin's Press, 1979.

Panek, LeRoy Lad. *Probable Cause: Crime Fiction in America*. Bowling Green: Bowling Green State University Press, 1990.

Rader, Barbara A., and Howard Z. Zettler. *The Sleuth and the Scholar: Origins, Evolution, and Current Trends in Detective Fiction*. New York: Greenwood Press, 1988.

BOOKS ON LITERATURE

Childers, Joseph, and Gary Hentzi. *The Columbia Dictionary of Modern Literary and Cultural Criticism*. New York: Columbia University Press, 1995.

Heise, Joris. *Literature: Discovering Ourselves through Great Books*. Boston: American Press, 1995.

Holland, Norman N. *The Dynamics of Literary Response*. New York: Oxford University Press, 1968.

Holman, Hugh C., and William Harmon. *A Handbook to Literature*, 6th ed. New York: Macmillan, 1992.

Jacobus, Lee A. *Literature: An Introduction to Critical Reading*. Upper Saddle River, N.J.: Prentice-Hall, 1996.

Murfin, Ross C. "The New Historicism and 'The Dead.' " *Case Studies in Contemporary Criticism: James Joyce "The Dead,"* ed. Daniel R. Schwarz. Boston: Bedford (St. Martin's Press), 1994.

Roberts, Edgar V., and Henry E. Jacobs. *Fiction: An Introduction to Reading and Writing*. Englewood Cliffs, N.J.: Prentice-Hall, 1987.

Showalter, Elaine, ed. *The New Feminist Criticism: Essays on Women, Literature, and Theory*. New York: Pantheon Books, 1985.

MISCELLANEOUS WORKS

Faulkner, William. "Nobel Prize Speech." Stockholm, 10 Dec. 1950.

U.S. Department of Justice Statistics. *Capital Punishment 1991*, Bulletin NCJ–136946. Washington, D.C.: U.S. Dept. of Justice, Oct. 1992: 7: Table 2.

Index

About the Author

MARY BETH PRINGLE is Professor of English at Wright State University in Dayton, Ohio, where she teaches modern/contemporary literature, women's studies, and writing. Her areas of professional interest include autobiography and personal writing by women and all facets of popular culture. She is coeditor of *The Image of Prostitute in Modern Literature* (1984) and *Sex Roles In Literature* (1980) and she is at work on *Approaches to Teaching Virginia Woolf's* To the Lighthouse. She has also published articles on a wide variety of popular culture topics.